MARRIAGE COMMUNICATION POWER
& SELF-HELP
FOR HIGH-CONFLICT COUPLES

**365 DAYS OF LOVE & RESPECT WITH YOUR PARTNER.
EFFECTIVE COUPLE SKILLS • CONFLICT RESOLUTION.
SET BOUNDARIES • MAKE MARRIAGE WORK.**

CAROLINE SOWLE

© Copyright 2022 Caroline Sowle - All rights reserved.

The content contained within this book may not be reproduced, duplicated or transmitted without direct written permission from the author or the publisher.

Under no circumstances will any blame or legal responsibility be held against the publisher, or author, for any damages, reparation, or monetary loss due to the information contained within this book, either directly or indirectly.

Legal Notice:

This book is copyright protected. It is only for personal use. You cannot amend, distribute, sell, use, quote or paraphrase any part, or the content within this book, without the consent of the author or publisher.

Disclaimer Notice:

Please note the information contained within this document is for educational and entertainment purposes only. All effort has been executed to present accurate, up to date, reliable, complete information. No warranties of any kind are declared or implied. Readers acknowledge that the author is not engaged in the rendering of legal, financial, medical or professional advice. The content within this book has been derived from various sources. Please consult a licensed professional before attempting any techniques outlined in this book.

By reading this document, the reader agrees that under no circumstances is the author responsible for any losses, direct or indirect, that are incurred as a result of the use of the information contained within this document, including, but not limited to, errors, omissions, or inaccuracies.

CONTENTS

Introduction	v
About the author	ix
1. WHAT IS MARRIAGE COMMUNICATION ANYWAY & WHY DO WE NEED IT?	**1**
Marriage as an Other	2
Common Types of Communication Within Marriage	3
Myths Surrounding Marriage	6
How Lack of Communication Will Affect Your Marriage	10
Chapter Summary	12
2. CORE CONFLICT	**13**
How Negative Communication Patterns Form	14
Identifying and Breaking Habits	15
Removing the Guesswork	18
Core Conflicts Couple Face	19
Don't Add Conflict to Conflict!	29
Chapter Summary	32
3. PRINCIPLES OF AN EFFECTIVE MARRIAGE	**33**
Tips for Conflict	34
Focus On Your Why	36
Time as a Commodity	48
Setting Healthy Boundaries	50
Your Basic Rights	54
Be Positive & Imagine Success	57
Chapter Summary	58
4. REAL LIFE EXAMPLES & SOLUTIONS	**59**
Fast Facts About Marriage	69
Can I Save the Marriage by Myself?	72
Chapter Summary	76

5. SO WHAT CAN YOU DO?	77
How to Make the Relationship 50% Better	78
Your Own Health in the Relationship	81
Self-Love Within a Marriage Is Not Selfish	84
The Way You Speak to Yourself Is How You Speak to Others	84
It's Harder to Love Yourself Than to Accept Love From Others	85
Learning to Be Your Own Best Friend	86
Quieting/Replacing Your Inner Voice	86
Make Time for You	87
Set Healthy Boundaries	87
Chapter Summary	88
6. MOVING FORWARD & MAINTAINING YOUR HEALTHY MARRIAGE	91
We Get What We Allow	94
How to Say Thank You	95
Benefits of Saying Thank You	96
Maintaining Without Arguing	98
Chapter Summary	99
Conclusion	101
Acknowledgments	105

INTRODUCTION

If we could all have the keys to a perfect and happy marriage, then life would be easy. But, sadly, this isn't always the case. If you are looking to improve your marriage, solve those conflicts that keep popping up, and implement techniques that are proven to work time and again, then you've come to the right place. We will take a realistic approach to problems that we all face in our marriage and find solutions that can be used time and time again.

Communication is a critical component at the base of all human interactions. Within a loving relationship, where children and other family members may be involved, communication can become even more important. It is essential to a functioning family dynamic.

The word communication evokes many thoughts such as simple speech, body language, tone of voice, etc. It will be useful to define the word communication in its most-used form, and we can therefore go on to explore its specific definition within marriage.

Communication: *a process by which information is exchanged between individuals through a common system of symbols, signs, or behavior.*

This definition works in many societies as people all over the world use different languages or behaviors to communicate with one another, but they are all ultimately for one reason which is to get a point across to someone else. With marriage, however, communication is used to ensure the emotional, physical, and mental needs of the bond of the marriage continue to be met. This definition can pertain to marriage in the sense that communication in marriage is absolutely a process! It will take time to rebuild the patterns you and your partner have slipped into.

If you are reading this book, you are most likely having a lapse in communication in one or several areas. And this is okay! Remember that we are all imperfect human beings. There are going to be times when it feels like everything goes smoothly and others when it will feel like you and your spouse may speak two distinct languages! But, this makes marriage so beautiful. The difficulties of the bond only work to make it strong as you and your partner travel rocky and smooth roads. You will find great companionship. This book can be your guide along the way.

We have many exciting things to discuss in the upcoming chapters. We will begin by defining several common types of communication in marriage and how the lack of these types will affect the marriage. I will do a bit of myth-busting! I will outline some common myths surrounding how a marriage should be, what it should look like, and show you the truth.

We will also spend some time on core conflicts couples face. Many couples face the same problems, although they may look different. Although at the core, they all stem from the same root! Defining these and understanding why they keep growing and popping up in your marriage will help squash them for good. Then, we will get to the proper stuff! We will discuss techniques that are proven to work and see some real-life examples in action.

Another important aspect we will learn together is how to improve the self. A marriage comprises two individual people. Before you can create unity with anyone else, you must be your person. Maybe there are things you know you need to work on that could improve your marriage situation this minute. We can identify some of these things, and they will only help in your communication with your partner.

After reading this book, I hope you'll be able to take away most or all of the following things:

- *A feeling of assurance that you and your spouse are not the only ones struggling*
- *A way to identify those core conflicts as soon as they pop up*
- *An understanding of how marriage communication is different & why it's so important*
- *Several principles & techniques for an effective marriage*
- *Steps to improve yourself in the marriage*
- *Confidence moving forward to maintain communication*

A healthy marriage is hard work. But when you have someone you love and want to be with for the rest of your life, the hard work is more than worth it. The payoff for learning to communicate effectively will have lifelong results.

ABOUT THE AUTHOR

With an academic degree in psychology, Caroline Sowle was faced with a choice not everyone has to make at such a tender age. Despite the fact she was offered a teaching position at a prestigious school, she decided relationship counseling was her life calling.

It's been 15 years since Caroline made her choice, and to date, she remains true to her mission. Although her beginnings were humble, nowadays she enjoys the well-deserved respect and appreciation of hundreds of people who she helped save their relationships.

Offering a powerful perspective and a unique skill set on finding and keeping a great relationship, Caroline helps couples make healthy, informed decisions in their love life. Rumor has it, love birds mentored by Caroline Sowle easily find their way to radiating their true colors and communicating their expectations effectively, minus the drama and otherwise inevitable conflicts.

Being at the forefront of transforming relationships for the better for more than a decade, Caroline is now referred to not only as a relationship expert, but also as a miracle worker. In her selfless efforts to help couples overcome difficulties, she is determined to publish her invaluable relationship guides.

Caroline's books and guides distill the thorough research and her extensive experience in the field of relationship counseling into life-changing insights and proven and practical solutions for finding common ground with the life partner.

In addition to a fruitful career, Caroline Sowle is recognized as the best mom and wife – according to her coffee mug!

https://www.facebook.com/carolinesowleauthor

1
WHAT IS MARRIAGE COMMUNICATION ANYWAY & WHY DO WE NEED IT?

After reading the introduction, you may think, *okay, I know what communication is now. Just tell me how to do it!* And, I promise I will (in Chapter 3) but we still have much to learn about how **marriage communication** differs. It is not quite the same as the communication we have defined in chapter 1.

Marriage communication is a collaborative effort, and the effects are damaging if it is not working. Instead of just working on your communication as a person, you have a whole other person and relationship to consider.

As an individual, we make choices every day. These choices directly affect how we view the world and how those view us. When in a marriage, the choices we make are not only affecting us but are affecting this. This is what we have built with our partner, this other thing. We could not have built this other thing without them. Throughout this book, I will reference marriage as an *Other*. Let me tell you what I mean by this.

Marriage as an Other

When we willingly enter a partnership, we become one with someone else. This partnership comprises two individual people who create something else, something else individual together. The marriage is a separate part of both people involved. So, in this sense, the two of you have created this *Other* thing together. It may seem like a marriage should be all-consuming, a complete part of you. And it should! Although, it should also be treated as a separate part of you, something that you continually have to work on, and should be proud to have built with your partner! You should still care about it just as much, but keep in mind that it is a separate part of yourself. Therefore, I reference it as an "Other". Because it is another part of you and your partner.

Work on it, give it attention, love, and appreciate it, or else it will go away. Marriages are more delicate than we realize! They are built on love and trust. This Other is something you have created with another person. It is something to be proud of! You have come this far and have decided that this Other part of you is something worth working on and improving.

Before we discuss marriage communication in more depth, let's first take a moment to acknowledge what you have already built with your spouse. This is a person who is there for you and you are there for them. Love is hard to find! This is a cliche, but cliches are just that for a reason. Because they are true! Give yourself a break at this moment. You have improved your situation within your marriage. Now that you see it for what it is, you can be grateful. Cultivating gratitude can be a great way to approach any kind of communication issue with a healthier and clear mind. If you are reading this, then it's clear that you care deeply for your partner and want to fix what isn't working! Communication can be tricky and change. Don't be discouraged because of a bump in the road.

Common Types of Communication Within Marriage

1. Spoken Communication

This seems like an obvious one! In a marriage, there is constant spoken communication going on. If you and your partner lead busy lives, this communication may be brief and therefore needs to be effective. More so than this, your spoken communication with your partner should be enjoyable! Many couples cite they were often best friends with their partner first.

Without comfortable spoken communications, there is no solid ground or no foundation for communication to grow on! Our spoken language is how many people in and out of relationships get their information to do just about everything in life. At the beginning of the marriage, the spoken communication is usually very high! You have been together for a while and know what works.

Communication seems easy, and you probably wonder how people have problems communicating within their marriage. But as time goes on, this may deteriorate because of additional responsibilities that come along with a marriage. This is a natural progression, but it doesn't mean that you can never get back to where you once were with your spoken communication abilities!

2. Nonverbal Expressions

Also known as body language, many couples can communicate solely through this avenue. Think about your relationship with your spouse and all the nonverbal cues you give each other.

Do you ever give your significant other a look or motion to them briefly while you are out in public, and magically, they somehow know exactly what you are saying? Humans have an innate ability to read one another's body language.

According to *Psychology Today*, the belief is that 55% of

communication is body language, 38% is the tone of voice, and 7% is the spoken word. This is such a high percentage of body language! 55% of all communication is over half of all languages. We are constantly giving off nonverbal cues, even without our conscious knowledge. It's good to be aware of this, especially when working on communication with your spouse. There will be moments when you feel frustrated and will outwardly show it before you state it verbally.

These interesting statistics do not pertain to married couples either but to people. I would guess that for married couples, the nonverbal expressions rank even higher.

When you are around someone all the time and get to know them, you gain a heightened ability to read them and know the things that will bother them without having to exchange actual words. This is an important skill, but one that needs to be noted. Our spouse is always sensing how we feel and picking up on things we do without us realizing it.

3. Emotional

Being in tune with your partner's emotions is crucial to a healthy marriage. If we cannot understand and empathize with how our partner is feeling, then how can we communicate about our needs and wants?

Some people are naturally more prone to anger or are more sensitive to comments. There's nothing wrong with this. At the core of most conflicts are emotions. Maybe we are feeling like our partner doesn't care about us and so we get upset about the laundry or the finances for that month.

Human beings seek emotional connection. We need it! Your partner is your go-to source for connection. They are the person who should be a safe person to talk to about your emotions. They should accept you no matter what you share with them. The world out there is tough enough, that's for sure. Your partner can be your sanctuary.

Effective emotional communication is critical because there will be times when your partner can sense you are feeling upset or angry. Then, both of you can adjust accordingly. This will be a crucial technique we will learn in Chapter 3. Communication and connection go hand in hand.

4. Touch

Physical affection is a way couples can share their emotions and deep connection with one another. Touch can be as simple as holding hands or as deep as sexual intimacy. Though original touch, both can be just as important to a marriage.

All people are unfamiliar with their preference for touch as well. Some like to be held more or have intimate connections more. This is important to know about your partner. If your partner likes to be held or maybe isn't into a public display of affections, that's okay. But it's good to communicate this to one another beforehand.

This type of communication can be used. *Have you ever had a bad day and your partner has been there to simply hug or kiss you? Did you have anxiety about an upcoming appointment and your spouse was there to hold your hand?*

These simple forms of communication toward touch can make all the difference in a marriage. They can be the difference between a present and non-present partnership. And we want to be as present as possible.

After all, being present is communication. We are deciding to be there and engage with our partner, whether it is verbally or nonverbally.

Myths Surrounding Marriage

Marriage can be a beautiful and sought-after experience. Although, for people who have been married for a long time, you know it's hard work! People who have not been married may not understand all the dedication and effort that goes into making this *Other* work.

Even if you have been married for a while, it's easy to look around at other couples and assume their life is easier than yours with your partner. Becoming so absorbed with the problems of your marriage can be detrimental. You will get fused within your relationship, assuming that everyone else is happy and you are the only two who aren't. But before you think this way, remember that the grass is always greener on the other side! When I think about it, I feel that I have always heard many myths surrounding marriage, and if you hear them enough, you may convince yourself they are real. However, it's critical to note that these are not genuine beliefs.

When you believe those myths, it's a great opportunity to access that gratitude we talked about. Many of these myths come from people who are absorbed in their conflicts or from people outside of the marriage itself. So before we can talk about common conflicts that plague most marriages at some point, it's important to discuss some myths surrounding marriages so we know what is real and not real before getting to the root issues.

Myth #1: Every Marriage is Perfect Except Mine

When things are going wrong in our life, it's difficult to not look around at other people and feel envious. Well, they look happy! But we never truly know what is going on in someone else's life, and especially in someone else's marriage. This is the whole "grass is greener on the other side mentality."

While this applies to all aspects of life, it is especially prevalent today because we can see parts of people's lives online. In today's time, social media is another big factor that contributes to this myth. It shows us only a small portion of someone's life.

We may see the Holiday photos or weekend trips that a "happy" family is taking together. This is only showing one side of the story. And I am not looking for negative aspects of those happy families, although it is good to take a realistic approach to other people, especially when your marriage may struggle with communication.

Try this exercise when you are struggling with this myth:

Think of something within your marriage that makes it imperfect. It could be something minor or something big. Do many people know about this? Do you post this on your Facebook? Remind yourself at this moment that all couples face issues and have problems they do not share with the outside world.

Myth #2: Your Partner Will Complete You

This is a myth that can be very damaging to romantic relationships. It's important to remember that no one can complete you! We have spoken about this Other thing which we can build together with our partner.

Looking for your other half is a positive thing, as long as that other half is going to add to the life you have already built for yourself. Before you can have a healthy partnership with anyone, whether it be a relationship or a marriage, you need to be a complete person by yourself.

If you can't love yourself and be happy alone, then you cannot put pressure on another person to fix that problem for you. It's not fair to them or you, and it puts an unnecessary strain on the relationship. While your spouse should complement your life and be your biggest supporter, they should not be what completes you. This can lead to **codependency,** which can be defined as the following:

- *a psychological condition or a relationship in which a person is controlled or manipulated by another who is affected by a pathological condition.*
- *broadly: dependence on the needs of or control by another.*

Codependency within romantic relationships is a common occurrence. Often it stems from relationship patterns that were based on codependency and even stems back to childhood. Many children who were codependent with their parents will seek similar romantic relationships in their adult life.

People will rely too much on their partner for emotional, physical, and mental support. Then, they cannot function alone. This is unhealthy for the relationship and can only have negative effects on communication patterns. We will discuss more codependency in Chapter 5.

Myth #3: Conflicts Only Come From Inside the Marriage

Conflicts can arise from any channel in a marriage. Outside sources such as job stress, family, friends can all bring conflicts. While we will discuss this Core Conflict more in the next chapter, it's shocking how much outside elements can infiltrate a fortunate marriage.

This isn't something we should aim to avoid, yet something we should aim to expect. In-laws, old friends, and family members who are always around can bring about problems that were never there, to begin with. But it's your job as one partner in the relationship to communicate and decide what you allow and don't allow into your relationship with your spouse. You do not always have to have an outward reaction to these things.

They are a distinct element of your relationship, but they are not part of your marriage. Arguments and disagreements are not always because of an intrinsic issue within the partnership. It also is not always a direct reflection of the two individuals.

Myth #4: Marriage Will Solve Problems Present Before the Marriage

I cannot stress enough how untrue this is! This connects back to codependency as well. Marriage is not a solution to relationship problems. Making a more serious commitment to solving core issues already present in the relationship can only cause them to become more ingrained. More problems arise once people get married. Without a firm foundation, the marriage cannot survive.

Marriage is not a magical problem-solver for issues that existed before entering the partnership. If you and your spouse already are facing problems before the marriage, the grass will not be greener on the other side! Communication will only falter more and more if it continues to be ignored. The proper work begins once marriage happens! It is a genuine commitment. You make the choice and promise to commit yourself to this Other thing and to be supportive to another individual.

Myth #5: Couples Counseling Is for People Who Are Going to Get Divorced

Couples counseling can be enormously helpful. If you have come to the point in your relationship where you realize you need additional help, this is nothing to be ashamed of or worried about.

When you are in a partnership, it's hard to have outside opinions that are not biased. Often we will ask our close family and friends their opinion on an argument or disagreement, and of course, they will take our side. Or, they may not offer advice as helpful as a professional. This is where good marriage counseling can be helpful.

A professional who specializes in communication and can see your conflicts from an unbiased view may just solve your problems. They can give you deeper techniques for communication and analyze the relationship from a new view.

Myth #6: Everything in a Marriage Must Be Equal

Now, this is just a hard standard to live up to. And I'm not sure many married couples feel this way. I'm sure a lot of women would say they do more blank and men would say they do more blank. An unequal marriage can make it work. For many couples, one spouse will work more, and this works for them individually as well because maybe they have a skill that allows them to make a steady income to provide for their family. And the other spouse will take care of the home or the children, or maybe pursue another venture.

Marriages are unequal in so many ways. About personality traits as well. As they say, opposites attract! What is the strength for one spouse may not be a strength for another. Maybe you are more empathetic and emotional in your relationship. You were there for your partner and know just what to say. Maybe your partner is more analytical and can solve problems that arise with finances or family situations. An Unequal marriage does not mean it is bad!

How Lack of Communication Will Affect Your Marriage

A lapse in communication will affect your marriage. It will lead to stress, unwanted emotions, and a feeling of distance between you and your spouse. We do not want this. Often there are things we want to say to our partner but we don't out of fear of the reaction or because we feel we are overreacting. But these things fester and become conflicts that do not go away. They sit right below the surface and will come out when we least expect them to. It's important to express our feelings. This also applies to all relationships but is true in marriage as your partner will be there for everything.

Misunderstandings and trust issues can grow from these conflicts. You may sense something is wrong with your spouse and wonder why they won't share with you. We all perceive situations differently, so if you and your spouse are not communicating directly, assumptions and misconceptions can easily happen. Suddenly, you find that you often become upset without knowing why or how it started. If they are not telling you their feelings, then you will feel confused about their perspective. If you are married, you care and trust this person, and somewhere along the line a lack of communication has caused this feeling to waiver.

This lack of proper communication can lead to feelings of loneliness. Your partner is someone you should be able to share both the good and bad things within your life. We can feel worse in an unhealthy relationship than we would be alone. I know this sounds sad! But take this book as your wake-up call. You want a change to happen and you want to better communicate with your spouse to improve trust from now on. Throughout this book, we will discuss how to be more open with your spouse, and how core conflicts from miscommunication can impede that. We will then talk about how we can work to strengthen the bond with our partner instead of making it weaker by not communicating how we feel.

If you are worried about how your partner will perceive these new communication techniques, that is completely normal. All change takes time, and you will have to be patient with both your spouse and yourself. We will go further and look at statistics on the reasons couples get divorced and the reasons they even get married in the first place so you can see that you are not alone in this!

Chapter Summary

- Marriage as a different communication: An Other
- Types of communication
- Common myths surrounding marriage

In the next chapter, you will learn the common conflicts surrounding marriage.

2

CORE CONFLICT

Regardless of what kinds of issues you and your partner face, they would probably look similar to another couple. Many people face these following problems in their marriage, but we don't always advertise it for the world to see. While issues take various forms, the core is the same. To understand any issues, we have to understand this!

This is a key part of the book as we will start at the beginning, identifying exactly what the problem is before we can even solve it. This is not a full list of all core problems, as each couple has its unique challenges. But let's work to cut these problems off at the root, and communicate better.

Even outside of our marriage, we will encounter conflict in our lives. It is a natural part of being human! When we are engaged in a partnership with another individual, we have to resolve this conflict. There is no option other than to resolve these problems because they will otherwise continue to fester within the relationship.

As an individual, we can choose to resolve a conflict or not, but once we are married, there is another person involved.

Maybe a better way to look at it is if you were having a problem at work or with a friend.

Would you like that problem to go unresolved? The answer is most likely no. But with those closest to us, we can sometimes forget the basics like communication! Communication is the first step to respect. Many of these issues have become habits we don't even realize we have formed.

How Negative Communication Patterns Form

As humans, we partake of inhabits every day. We do little things similarly every morning when we first wake up and we do the same thing before bed each night. We have patterns of thinking that become habitual, and we can also form habits within our social relationships.

Try to identify some patterns or habits that you and your partner have. *Does one of you make breakfast for you both? Who wakes up first? If you have children, who brings them to school?* These are all patterns that are formed through communication. Many of these may have been formed over time, with no verbal communication at all. You may have fallen into these patterns with your partner, just automatically knowing what works best for the both of you. Without effective communication, these habits simply wouldn't happen.

For those who are closest to us, such as our spouse, there are already these habitual patterns in place. Over time, these may grow and change into something more positive or negative. If you are here, you may have noticed certain communication in your marriage going in a negative direction. This is okay. It is never too late to break a habit and replace it with a new, more positive one. While we cannot always pinpoint an exact moment a habit was formed, we can see a pattern once it is there.

Habitual patterns within relationships take time to form, just like habits do. It's like the familiar saying that it takes 21 days to make or break a habit! If within your marriage you are repeatedly miscommunicating, having the same arguments, and not listening to one another, these are negative communication patterns. Out of these patterns come core conflicts that will arise each time there is a lack of communication.

Now try to identify some negative patterns that have formed. *Do you leave your clothes lying around all over the place, and your spouse always asks you to pick them up? Have you stopped doing those weekly dinner dates with your partner? Do you wish there was more intimacy in your relationship but you don't talk about it anymore?*

Whatever the context, there are good and bad habits scattered throughout our marriage. Do you see how the habit takes many forms, but at the core, they are still negative habits? This is much like the core conflicts we will get into. They take on unfamiliar faces, but underneath it is all the same. We want to identify those habits so we can decide if we want to keep them or not from now on.

Identifying and Breaking Habits

So how do you know if that's an unpleasant habit or not that you do in your relationship? If you have to ask, then it may not be the healthiest. We know some positive ones such as always doing the laundry at the same time each week so it is ready, cleaning off the bathroom sink, cleaning the dishes, making sure there is enough coffee for your spouse in the morning when they wake up, etc.

These are all actions that prevent conflict and may even bring a sense of appreciation to your marriage. If you notice something you are doing is causing you and your partner unhappiness instead of appreciation, then that is a pretty solid giveaway! But these things can be difficult to notice at the moment, and we don't always see it right away that a bad habit is forming until it's already in place.

Once you take the time to reflect and have identified something that isn't healthy for you or your marriage, what is the next step? Here are a few things I have found useful within my marriage and things I have seen other couples do to help them get back on the right track.

1. Make Small Changes at a Time

Basically, don't go cold turkey! Things we are used to doing won't just go away. They take time to form and will take an equal amount of time to go away. Be patient with yourself and give yourself a little leeway.

If the habit is something like never doing the laundry, try doing one load of laundry a week. This may help your spouse out even just a little and I'm sure that they will appreciate the effort. For most things in life, it is the little things that really can make a difference.

2. Make a Plan

Are you going to break this habit in a month, 6 months, a year? Whatever you decide to do, and depending on how big of an issue the habit is, stick to it. Write it down. Write it on your phone or on a piece of paper and carry it around with you. This will make it harder for you to forget about it and brush it off when you have to get to work on it.

You want to stay consistent because habits need consistency, whether they are good or bad. They are an action that is repeated over and over until it sticks! So, for you to get that healthy habit to stick, keep at it.

3. Plan For Mistakes

Breaking a habit is hard work and it won't all be easy. You will mess up, and you will have to start over. That's okay! Sometimes it won't stick, and you will have to start over. There is a learning curve to everything. But if you start with the right mindset and plan for this, you won't be as hard on yourself when the time comes that you have a misstep.

Planning for mistakes is also a way to prepare yourself for if it happens. While it's not a guarantee that it will happen, being prepared for anything can keep you from taking it too hard. You don't want to get so down on yourself that you decide to give up completely on changing the negative habit.

4. Tell Your Partner You Are Making a Change

This isn't necessary to show off to them (although it will look good) it's for support! Telling your partner you are making a positive change will show them you care about the relationship and want the best for the both of you.

Whenever we are making any kind of change in our life, having people who love and care for us in our corner can make all the difference. It can be the difference between whether we succeed. This can be especially helpful if your spouse knows you are working on the relationship! It may even motivate them to change a habit that they have within the marriage that has been bothering you.

5. Identify Those Triggers

If there is something that makes you engage in a bad habit, note this. Sometimes, sadly, a habit cannot be broken until we realize why we are even engaging in this habit. Triggers may be something small or big that stops us from achieving what we want. They can be a distraction or another bad coping mechanism preventing us from moving in a good direction. Negative things that trigger us have to be removed from the situation for us to achieve.

6. Find an Alternative

So you're giving one thing up, but maybe you want to adopt a different, more positive habit. Say you are trying to drink less. Maybe instead, have a piece of chocolate or another treat that you like. Of course, we won't want to indulge too much, but this can be a suitable replacement for the time being. It's not good to restrict yourself too much while making a big change.

Focus your mind on the one big habit you want to break. This way, you are not overwhelming yourself. If you find yourself too overwhelmed, it might tempt you to give up. You also might find that the reason you are engaging in one behavior might be out of comfort or because of anxiety etc. and it can easily be replaced with a healthier, more positive habit.

Breaking habits is no fun. When you have to do so for the sake of your relationship, it can be even more difficult. But think of all the benefits! Don't you want your relationship to be as healthy as possible so that you can work on your communication?

We will talk in Chapter 5 about becoming the best version of ourselves for our relationship to benefit. Taking care of our individual emotional, mental, and physical health will add to the overall health of our marriage. Breaking negative habits is a great way to begin this process.

Removing the Guesswork

It can be exhausting when you and your partner are no longer communicating like you used to. Maybe you were reading this book because you and your spouse had great communication at one point and now you're thinking, what happened? Some time passes and you're thinking, *did I do something? Did they do something? Who is at fault here?*

Usually, in miscommunication scenarios, no one person is at fault. Things get lost in translation, and every person has a fresh perspective so it is natural for misunderstandings to happen. People who have been married for a long time tend to fall into a comforting routine. They may assume their partner is always on the same page as them. But that routine can take away things like emotional honesty, open conversation, and intimacy. In the space that was left behind, you will find lots of guessing.

Have you ever been in a situation outside of your marriage where you genuinely were confused? Maybe this was at work when you were assigned a new project or when you were younger in school and there was a new subject you just couldn't understand. What did you do in that situation? I bet you asked for help! This book can be a version of that for you! I am glad you are reaching out for help in this way, as we can go through this process together. But remember, you ultimately will have to reach out to your partner. That is the last step in this process.

No one wants to be guessing in their marriage! Especially after you've decided this is the person you want to be with, maybe have children with, and share the rest of your life with. Who has time to guess? Things should be communicated naturally and easily, right? Wrong. It happens all the time. We assume things are good just because we are married. But we can't possibly have all the answers. And that is because we are separate individuals!

Understanding these conflicts can help remove the guesswork. It takes away the questioning we do to try to figure things out. *Are these conflicts coming from outside sources? Or are they within your marriage?* Wherever they are coming from, directly communicating and solving them together will lead you and your partner to a more trusting and loving partnership.

Core Conflicts Couple Face

We are now ready to talk about the different core conflicts you may face in your marriage. This list compiles some of the most common conflicts, although it will not cover them all of course. Every marriage is different, and the conflicts you face throughout your time together will change and take different forms. Hopefully, you can find similarities in your relationship.

As you read through, try comparing them to situations you and your spouse have been through. Use the examples as a guide for the way you may behave in situations as well. Recognizing you are not alone in these struggles can already ease some of your anxiety.

1. Not Listening

One of the most common issues I hear repeatedly is that one partner feels their other partner just isn't paying attention to them. *An attentive partner is a loving partner.* Most of us truly just want to feel like our partner cares and wants to be there. We want them to want to be there! It is frustrating when your spouse constantly is missing things and you feel you can never grab their attention. This is a clear communication breakdown. There are countless examples of this, but here is one in which the communication loss happens because of the couple being engaged in things other than each other.

Ben is watching football on Sunday afternoon. His wife, Jill, needs to know whether he will pick up their son from school on Monday. She calls his name several times and eventually uses nonverbal cues to get his attention, waving to him and eventually standing in front of the T.V.

She asks him if he will pick up Carter from school the next day because she will be at work. He nods his head and motions for her to get out of the way. Ben rarely listens when watching T.V. and will prioritize it over his wife. The next day, Ben forgets Jill asked him to pick Carter up.

This is such a frustrating scenario for many couples. How many times have you tried to have a necessary conversation with your spouse and feel they are not listening at all? These kinds of situations happen all the time in marriages, taking various forms.

Maybe something needs to be done around the house or a bill needs to be paid. Whatever the issue is, I'm sure this conflict is recognizable and relatable for many people.

2. Nagging

Does your partner always ask you to do things? Does it feel like they are more like your boss than your spouse? This can happen over time with a marriage. People get comfortable and reliant on one another to where nagging easily comes into play. One partner may end up doing most of the work and the other gets comfortable with this. They like being taken care of while the other one acts as the caretaker.

Maybe you are the one who does the nagging in the relationship, or maybe you are the one being told what to do. Either way, it's not a fun time. This is a conflict that can easily become obnoxious for both parties involved and is very damaging for communication overall.

Angela hates when her husband wears his shoes in the house. He comes inside one evening wearing them. She says, "Can you please take your shoes off?" Her husband groans and takes them off. But, he leaves them in the living room. An hour later, Angela noticed the shoes downstairs in the living room and asked him to put them away.

He said that he will. After dinner, the shoes were still there. She asked him again. Finally, before bed, the shoes were still there, and Angela picked them up herself and put the shoes away.

As stated, neither person in this scenario is having a good time. Angela doesn't like that she has to keep nagging her husband, and he doesn't enjoy being nagged! With proper communication, this wouldn't be a problem. Not only does her husband feel like she is nagging, but Angela most likely feels that he is not present. He does not even seem to acknowledge her as she asks him several times, and he still does not put his shoes away.

3. Bringing up the Past

This is such a detrimental conflict for any romantic relationship, but especially in a marriage. In a marriage, you're there for the long haul! You are together for life. The decision has been made to put everything behind you and move forward in life together. At least, this decision is assumed to have been made.

Therefore, if you make the conscious choice to forgive your spouse for something, you cannot continue to bring it up in future arguments. This will only cause more resentment and will lead to no resolution. It's also exhausting to have the same arguments day after day. Deciding to forgive is free for both you and your spouse. Everyone is human and will make mistakes. Marriage is a partnership and a learning experience. It will not all go smoothly.

Lisa's husband has lied to her in the past. They have mostly been minor lies, although they have bothered her. The two spoke about it and resolved. He has not lied to her since. They are now having a conflict over Lisa's inability to be on time. During an argument over Lisa's habit of being late, she says, "Well, you are a liar!"

In this situation, it was completely unfair for Lisa to call her husband a liar. While it's true, he has lied to her in the past; they have moved on from that now and are arguing about something unrelated. By bringing this backup, she is deflecting from the genuine conflict and blame-shifting. She is also going back on her agreement to forgive and move forward.

Their argument was not even about her husband's behavior but was instead about her being late. This can only cause more of an issue. She needs to simply accept responsibility for her behavior and actively work to change it.

4. Finances

Money is the root cause of countless problems. It is stressful!

Paying bills and worrying about finances puts strain on a relationship. When you enter a marriage, your finances become entangled. Then, if you have children, there is even more stress surrounding money. You have to pay for clothes, food, schooling, and eventually a college fund! Ah! I am getting stressed right now, thinking about it all.

Rachel has been putting most of her paycheck away so she and her husband can save up for a house. She finds out that Rick has been spending money on new, expensive sneakers. When she confronts him, he tells her he works hard for his money and he can do whatever he wants with it. This upsets Rachel because she wants to buy a house and have children with Rick, but she feels he is only using his money for himself.

In a partnership, think of more than just yourself. In this scenario, Rick is only thinking of his wants and needs. Though he knows Rachel wants to buy a house with more space so they can have children, he wants new sneakers! This is a clear conflict and many couples go through this. Agreeing about your wants and goals will ensure that for finance, you and your spouse will be in line with how you handle money.

5. In-Laws

Do you love your wife/husband, but hate your in-laws? This happens often. It can cause many arguments and fights, especially if your spouse loves to be around or have their family in your home. Your spouse may want their family around all the time, but you just can't stand having them there. Perhaps they are loud, invasive, rude, etc. It doesn't matter. To you, your partner may be so different from their family. You may wonder how they even tolerate them! Or, you may be on the other side. Maybe you love your family, but it's your partner who can't stand them. Similar to the Nagging conflict, this is not an ideal situation for either party involved.

Erin's birthday is coming up, and her mother and father want to come to visit from Florida. Her husband, John, doesn't like them. He thinks they are very critical of people and would prefer if they stayed in a hotel. Erin disagrees because she feels if they stay in a hotel then she will have less time to see them and they cannot see their grandkids as much.

For this kind of situation, often a sacrifice has to be made. John should put his feelings aside and allow Erin's parents to stay in their home. Although, every situation is unique. And depending on what was said in the past, he may not want them in his home. This is understandable. This is a crucial situation where communication is needed.

The choices that are made here will not only affect the two people in the marriage but will extend to Erin's parents and her and John's children as well. The kids may wonder why their grandparents aren't staying with them. Proper communication between both Erin and John and then communication with their children will help make this situation better.

6. Friends

As we have talked about, each person in the marriage is a separate individual. So, before the marriage, you each led separate lives! This means you have had previous relationships and friends that you knew before your spouse even came into the picture. This is completely healthy, and these relationships should be maintained even once you and your partner are married.

People outside the marriage can interfere and cause conflict. Friends, especially, as they will influence the way you think and behave towards certain situations in your marriage. I would like to look at two specific examples for this conflict.

George and Anne have been married for two years now. George has had a good friend, Olivia, since he was in college. Lately, Anna has noticed that George and Olivia have been texting and talking on the phone more often than usual. When she confronts him about it, he tells her she is just a good friend and that there is nothing to worry about.

Isabelle and her best friend Rose always see each other. They often hang out on the weekend. They will grab drinks or dinner. Rose will come over to Isabelle's house during the week as well, and they will have movie nights, dinner, etc. Isabelle's husband feels he does not get enough time with her as she is always with Rose. He expresses this to her, and she says she will attempt to be with him more. When Isabelle tells Rose what her husband said, Rose tells her he is overreacting.

Both scenarios about friendship are unique but happen all the time in marriages! In the first situation, Anne has a right to be questioning why George is speaking to Olivia more. We all have a past, and we bring baggage to a marriage! This can come as past relationships that have done a real number on us, or as friends that may have a secret romantic interest in us. While Anne is not bringing up the past here, she is instead setting a proper boundary for her marriage and asking about a relationship that is affecting her marriage. George needs to listen to what his wife is saying and the two need to communicate about the situation with Olivia better.

In the second scenario, Isabelle is prioritizing her friendship over her marriage. She even tells her friend Rose that her husband would like to spend more time together, and Rose diminishes it. A good friend would not behave this way. They would want the best for both you and your marriage! Remember, your partner always comes first! Isabelle and her husband are not communicating effectively on this issue, as she continues to put Rose first.

7. Career

This specific conflict often goes hand in hand with finances. Each marriage is unique. But in some, one person is the "breadwinner" in the sense that they bring home most of the money. Their career pays the bills, takes care of groceries and transportation. The other partner may raise the children or contribute in another way. Either way, both roles in the marriage should be respected. Each partner brings something unique, and if you have entered a partnership with this person, then the roles should be discussed and communicated properly.

Charlotte has been a lawyer for years. She makes a lot of money, but she also works long hours and two weekends a month. She and Tim have only been married for two years. He only works part time, and she, therefore, brings in most of the money. She pays for the mortgage, car payments, and more. She wants him to get a full-time job and help with some payments, although Tim does not see a reason for it. Charlotte is feeling frustrated because she works extremely hard for her money.

Some couples are okay with one person making more money than another. Others need to split the work equally. In this situation, Charlotte is feeling like she works much harder than Tim and would like him to contribute more. He doesn't see the need because she makes so much. But, she works for that money! Charlotte will need to communicate this to Tim for their marriage to work.

8. Arguing Over One Another

When you are married, verbal fights will happen. They just will! All kinds of arguments will happen. But nothing productive can come of this if you and your partner are simply screaming over one another. The effective way to avoid arguing is to take turns expressing your feelings. But arguing over each other is so common within marriages, as both people want to get their point across. This creates an unhealthy environment and makes no space for true communication to happen.

Mark promised to show up to Alyssa's work dinner, but he did not show. They have only been married for a short time, and this was the first time she was going to introduce him to her colleagues. Alyssa felt let down and embarrassed when he did not show up. When she called him, he was still at his office, working.

Later that night, when Alyssa and Mark were both home, they got into a yelling match about it. Mark screamed that it wasn't a big deal, and he had to work to help support them, and Alyssa was screaming about how it embarrassed her. Both were trying to get their point across that neither one could listen to the other.

This is a classic scenario in which both partners believe they are right. Mark forgot about the dinner because he was working, and Alyssa was furious because he did not show. She was embarrassed in front of her colleagues, but Mark felt he had a good enough excuse to not show.

Instead of talking this out logically, the two screamed at each other. Strangely, the screaming does show that they care and are passionate about their point of view, but how can they possibly get this point across to one another? Nothing was resolved, and they both went to bed, harboring resentment over the situation.

9. Intimacy

Couples will go through periods where sex is great and where it is just not so great. This is a natural part of being a human as well. Just like Touch communication, sex will be more important for some partners than it will be for others. It's good to know where your spouse stands on this. Have candid conversations! Ask them what they think:

How much would you like to have sex? Is there anything else you would like to try? Do you feel connected to me when we are intimate?

After marriage, intimacy may take a backseat. Other important things may become a priority. But human touch is another way we communicate with one another, and it is how we can show our spouses we love them. Of course, things like doing the dishes or taking the kids to practice when it's not our turn is a great way to show them, but becoming intimate with our partner is a different level of connection.

Humans crave connection and intimacy is a primary component of this connection. Sex is important for a variety of reasons, some of them being: a chance to bond with your partner, a stronger sense of security in the relationship, love, and affection, and fun! Intimacy is also a way to enjoy your partner and spend time with them. It is something fun and pleasurable the two of you can engage in together.

10. Avoidance

An issue at the base of all these other issues may be avoidance. When we aren't communicating with our partners, we are avoiding something. The "elephant in the room" feeling is terrible. It's incredible how long couples can go without talking about something. But this is terrible, and no way to live in a committed relationship with your partner.

We don't want to avoid issues because then they will fester and pop up again. We can't ignore problems, especially in our marriage. It's important to identify what's bothering us, communicate it to our spouse, deal with it, and move on. If we avoid it, we are compromising our values and feelings, which can lead to lower self-esteem and bitterness towards our spouse.

Lily hates when her husband texts his friends during their movie night. One day a week, she and Tom watch a movie, but he is always texting his friends during it. She says nothing though because she doesn't want to start an argument. One weekend, the two go out to a fancy dinner. Tom texts in the middle of the meal and Lily yells at him in the middle of the restaurant. All of her frustration built up finally comes out.

By holding back her feelings, Lily only lets them bubble up inside. Tom didn't know she disliked him texting during their movie nights and so he continued to do it. He even texted during a nice dinner. This caused Lily to finally snap. This is what we want to avoid in our relationships. We don't want these moments where we snap! By communicating instead of avoiding, we can stay clear of this situation. In most areas of life, we will get what we allow! This is something we will discuss more in Chapter 6, but noting the behaviors we allow in our life can help us recognize those same behaviors within our marriage.

Hopefully, some of these conflicts and situations were relatable for you. They can seem overwhelming and you may wonder how you can get over all these obstacles. But it is possible! Identifying the problem and the root issues allows us to have a starting point. We will now take these conflicts and learn principles and techniques for how to overcome them. These issues do not have to be the end of your marriage and they do not have to control your relationship. Patience is key. These negative habits took time to form and they will take time to break. These unhealthy communication patterns will improve one step at a time!

Don't Add Conflict to Conflict!

Sometimes we can see these conflicts at play. But that doesn't always mean we will work on them. As humans, we do all kinds of strange things to ignore what is happening!

Decide now to *stop adding conflict to conflict*. If you're wondering what this means, there are several ways we can make the core conflicts in our marriage worse. Let's look at some of these ways.

General Avoidance

This is the final core conflict and can come in many forms. *Has your partner ever tried to discuss with you what's happening but you just won't hear it?* This is not helpful for you or the relationship, because if you will not work on the problem then how is it going to get fixed?

Avoidance can also pertain to not expressing feelings altogether. Then, they build up so much that one partner explodes. Instead of discussing the conflict in a calm and useful way, the partner will yell or become argumentative. Avoidance does nothing but leads to a bigger problem. We want to "avoid" avoidance!

Need to Be right

Our ego gets the best of us all sometimes. But as humans, we can't always be right! Especially in our relationships, we need to compromise and admit when we are at fault. Otherwise, our communication will suffer without a doubt.

A huge part of marriage is compromising and making the conscious choice to put our partner's needs before our own. During arguments, we will have the decision to make whether we want to be right or whether we want to make up.

Being Too Defensive

Talking through conflict and figuring out what the root issue is is just a healthy part of marriage. It is necessary to trust your partner and overcome problems. If you become too defensive, nothing will be solved. No one is perfect, and we have to accept our flaws.

When we enter a partnership with another, we are choosing to accept their flaws! And they are accepting ours. Therefore, we don't need to be defensive when our partner wants to talk about issues together and come up with the best solutions. They know who we are and have decided we are the person they want to be with from now on. Therefore, it is a positive thing for them to want to discuss issues and work them out with us.

The Blame Game

This goes hand in hand with being too defensive. We are all to blame! In a partnership, it takes two to tango! Of course, in some situations, one person may be more at fault. But this can be communicated healthily and positively.

We don't want to yell at our partner or point fingers but look for positive solutions together. Even if one person is at fault, the two of you can work together to fix the problem and get back to trust.

Character Attacks

Have you ever gone after your partner's character during an argument instead of addressing the conflict? This is extremely unhelpful. It's unhealthy to associate your partner's mistakes with their inner being!

They are two different things. No one's mistakes make up who they are as a person. We all do things that do not align with our values and true self. But that doesn't mean the people in our life should write us off and attack us.

Sweeping Generalizations

Try to avoid phrases like "you never" or you always. These phrases are not accurate and generalize every situation. Each argument and issue is different. The conflicts you and your partner face will change and take different forms.

Before you generalize a situation, try to think about if it's true. This type of issue often goes hand-in-hand with character attacks. When you generalize something, you may summarize someone's character altogether and paint them in a negative light.

This chapter may have been overwhelming on conflicts, as we spoke a lot about the issues you will face with your partner and may already be facing. But don't be discouraged!

In the next chapter, we will talk in-depth about ways you can overcome these core conflicts. There are many moving parts to a marriage, and it takes time for a change. These core conflicts build over time and will therefore take just as much time to get rid of!

We will talk about the principles to strengthen your communication, and then we will get into real-life examples of these principles in action.

Chapter Summary

- How negative patterns form
- Core conflicts couples face
- Examples of couples who are dealing with conflict

In the next chapter, you will learn principles to strengthen your communication and build trust.

3

PRINCIPLES OF AN EFFECTIVE MARRIAGE

Now that we have identified common conflicts and ways that we can make the conflicts worse, it's time to tackle them! This is an exciting chapter! We are learning how to improve our overall relationship with our partners. While this book is primarily about effective communication with your spouse, these techniques can apply to any social relationship. Because of this, this is arguably the most important chapter in this book. We will go through some principles that are proven to be effective when dealing with conflict in marriage.

I have composed a 10-Principle guide that you can use whenever you feel necessary. We will talk about the **STRENGTHEN 10-Principle Guide** that you can follow during any conflict you may face in your marriage.

This guide will help you in any core conflict you encounter with your spouse. You can keep this book with you in your dresser, car, purse, anywhere! It will come in handy when you realize you are at a crossroads and your communication could either suffer or improve, depending on your response.

We will go through the steps, but before we can do so, let's look at a couple of tips to help you get in the right mindset to deal with a discussion with your partner. We have talked a great deal about perspective, and how this can change the way we react or don't react to situations with our partner. You want to make sure you are looking through a positive lens to make a change. These tips will help "set the stage" for conflict resolution.

Tips for Conflict

The way you and your partner dealt with this disagreement or argument can be an enormous factor in whether it gets resolved. Attitude is everything! The solution can be in the approach! Before we get into the nitty-gritty, if you will, we want to look at our approach from an outside perspective and see if we are cultivating a positive environment to have a discussion. These tips will help you set the stage for a productive discussion. While there are plenty of other ways you can cultivate a good mindset, these are some ones that have proven to be most effective.

1. Stay Calm!

This sounds easier than it is. We cannot simply "stay calm" at all times. If we could, I think life would be much easier! During discussions with your partner, things will get heated naturally. Both sides will want to express how they feel, and this is completely normal. It means the two of you truly care for one another. You want your partner to understand why you are behaving the way you are. Why bother fighting with someone you don't care about? An interesting take on it. But, it is better to stay calm, especially when deciding to resolve a *core conflict*.

These are the conflicts you find coming up repeatedly, and if they are not approached healthily and respectfully, then the conversation is doomed from the beginning. Remember why you had this discussion. Remaining calm and steadfast in your decision to resolve this issue will keep your mind focused on the right issue.

2. Keep Your Eyes Open for "Middle Ground"

Often couples will find that they feel the same way towards a situation but are having a different reaction to it. Do you and our partner ever both feel disrespected? Or maybe you both feel you aren't spending enough time together, but you express this in different ways. One partner may cry and the other may get angry. A lapse in communication will create this confusion.

When you decide to have an honest and open discussion with your partner, you may find lots of similarities! Compromising will be a key factor to these principles, and looking out for any aspects that you and your partner may share in can fast-track you to success. Compromising means you may have to set aside something to solve an argument. But we do this throughout our marriage. We have to sacrifice for the *Other* to benefit.

3. Choose Your Battle

Before you even decide to engage in a discussion with your significant other, be sure that it's worth it! We can fight over such minute things, and the battle isn't necessary. Ask yourself, what will come of this? Will our relationship truly improve from having this discussion?

If this is something that doesn't matter to your relationship, consider letting it go. Don't let your ego get the best of you. Although, when we hold things inside instead of being open and honest with our partner, it becomes easy to blow up over little things. If these little things have a more serious, underlying core conflict, then this is a worthy discussion! But being able to decipher between the two can save you from a lot of unnecessary disagreements.

4. Pick an Open & Welcoming Environment

You want to find a neutral place to discuss these situations with your partner. An example of a bad environment would be out at dinner with friends. We will discuss this further in the "Good Timing" principle. But, dinner with friends is probably not the most appropriate time to discuss something that is bothering you! With people around, you will be worried about judgment, and it is not an appropriate time to discuss things that are sensitive to your relationship.

You and your partner know the full story, but not everyone around you does. You do not need other people to feel they can add their input. There is a time and place for everything, especially in a marriage. Be sure that you are somewhere the two of you can discuss openly and honestly with one another.

Focus On Your Why

You have your tips ready to go, and we are about to talk about the **STRENGTHEN** guide. But, *why is it you want to work on your marriage?* This is a big question, and it's important to keep in mind as we work through this book. Is your partner important to you? Do they add value to your life, and do you add value to theirs?

Surely our partners add some kind of value to our life, otherwise, we wouldn't care for them so much or want to strengthen our bond. We all have a deeper reason for doing anything in life, and tapping into this can give us an even bigger reason to do so. You have worked on your communication and read these techniques, so there is something in you that wants a change. And a positive one! Here are some questions to ask yourself:

- *Do you want to feel more connected to your partner?*
- *Are you looking to better understand their perspective?*

- *What is it that you value about your partner so much that you will work on your marriage?*
- *Do you care about your partner's feelings?*

There could be a million more reasons you are looking to improve your marriage. Only you know the true reason. Maybe there are other people involved, such as children. Whatever your reason is, make sure you identify it so that you can focus on it throughout this guide. This will also help you get into the right mindset while going through the principles. It will set you up for success. Remember, this is all about strengthening your marriage and communication!

We will follow the **STRENGTHEN 10-Principle Guide** to stop fights and build trust. These principles do not have to be followed in any order, but they can be used. I have used several of these at once and sometimes I only need one to solve a conflict! Every marriage is different, and there is no wrong way to go about learning these principles.

Read through these principles with an open mind. Be sure to only follow the ones that align with your values! If you feel a particular principle will not work for your marriage or your person, that's okay!

These are principles I have seen in action, and that I have often used myself. Each person will chart their path to healthier communication within their marriage. Remember to be patient with yourself and your partner and focus on why you have worked on your marriage.

Statements

The way we talk to one another can determine the way we resolve any conflict in our marriage. *Do you blame your partner? Do you tell them what they need to be doing differently? Or maybe they do this to you.* Either way, we want to shift away from using the word "you" and instead of using "I statements." Being intentional about how we speak will instantly help communications.

These "I statements" will come up several times throughout this book. Often we simply aren't aware of the words we say to our partner. We get comfortable around them and do not even know that what we are saying is affecting our relationship negatively. There is nothing wrong with being comfortable around our partners, but we still need to be intentional about how we speak to them.

When we become intentional with our words, the awareness automatically follows. We notice how we speak to our partners and how they respond to it. "I statements" are often better than " You statements," as they are less accusatory. "You statements" feel more like an attack and will not make your partner feel like they are in a safe environment to discuss openly.

For example: Instead of *"You never listen to me when I need you,"* try *"I feel upset when you don't listen to me. It makes me feel you don't care."* and instead of *"You don't spend time with me anymore."* try *"I miss our time together. Can we schedule some time this week for you just?"*

Using "I statements" is a great way to shift the blame away from your partner and instead healthily express your feelings. Expressing is so crucial. This way, your partner can empathize with the way you are feeling instead of feeling attacked. They can hear your needs without feeling defensive. When put on a defense, our partner may get angry.

We want to avoid anger at all costs when communicating. Anger does nothing but cloud judgment and prevents us from building trust. Have you ever heard the phrase *"seeing red?"* This is referencing when someone becomes so angry that their face becomes red and they can see nothing else. We want to avoid this at all costs in our marriage. Seeing things clearly, and being able to empathize with our partner, will help build connection and trust.

Tone of Voice

Similar to the words we speak, the delivery of those words can be just as important. Sometimes it's not so much what we say, but the way it is delivered. The tone of voice refers to how you speak your works and the impression it has on the surrounding people. You may say one thing, but your tone says another. There are a few different aspects to your tone of voice to look out for! Noting this, especially during an argument, can help de-escalate any situation.

Pitch

This refers to how high or low you speak. Do you usually speak in a high-pitched or low-pitched tone of voice? If this is altered during an argument, your partner will most definitely notice. Most people are somewhere in between. If you speak in a high pitch when you normally don't, it may appear defensive or untruthful. Many people have a higher tone of voice when they lie.

If you speak low, you may sound more serious. While everyone will interpret this differently, being aware of this will help you know the reaction from your spouse. You want to control the way you sound and make sure you are giving off the right pitch.

Pace

How quickly or slowly you speak. I have friends who speak super quickly naturally. During a discussion with your spouse, slowly down can calm a situation, especially if you and your partner are in a heated argument. When you get nervous, do you speed up your speech? I know I do this. You may find that you speed up your speech even when you have a discussion. Having a discussion is a lot like being put on a podium.

Speaking low gives a different feel. However, if you speak too slow, it may seem condescending. You want to speak evenly and calmly so that your partner can understand what you are saying, but not in a demeaning manner. Speaking too slowly can make your partner feel you are talking down to them. Being attentive to your pace will already help you focus more on your partner because you are listening to your voice and to what you are communicating to them.

Volume

This may seem like an obvious one! But during a heated discussion, we do not always consider how loud we are speaking. You and your partner may raise your voice naturally without realizing it. Make sure you are not escalating to where you are talking over your spouse.

Also, arguments can get out of hand and become unsafe when spouses yell and scream. You also want to consider other people that may live in the house, such as family members and children. If you are yelling over your partner, no one will communicate anything, and you definitely will not be listening to them.

Timbre

This refers to the emotional quality of your tone. Do you seem like you care? Do you seem disinterested or are you responding emphatically to what they say? We can perceive all different emotions in the tone of someone's voice. Your partner will react to the quality of emotion in your tone. They will tell if you are truly listening and understanding what they are saying.

We pick up on more than we realize and being aware of how

our partner will receive our speech can make any discussion go more smoothly. Our spouses can sense we are upset before we even tell them. Our tone of voice will give this away. The same sentence can sound different depending on how you say it.

For example: *Say your spouse asks if you would like them to take out the trash. You say, "Yes, it needs to go out" in an annoyed tone. They may feel confused because you are responding positively to their question, yet they can tell you are upset by your tone.*

If we step back for a moment and think of the benefits of speaking in a negative tone, there are none. Your partner will probably still take out the trash and the chores will still get done. Using a negative tone of voice will not speed up this process. But if you do, now you are both feeling annoyed, as your partner certainly won't appreciate your tone of voice. Your partner may not have been aware that you were feeling annoyed, and they may be confused about why you were annoyed.

Therefore proper communication is so important because the tone of voice can mislead in so many ways. Instead of expressing directly, a negative tone of voice will do the same thing, but indirectly! We want to break down this habit of indirect communication.

Really Listen!

Truly listening to our spouse is harder than it seems. We may assume we already understand them and know all there is to know about them! This can lead to miscommunication and assumptions, which are never good. People are constantly growing.

Every person is unique and while we can certainly know more than the average person about our partner, we cannot possibly know it all! Listening without getting defensive is also crucial to working on conflicts. We don't want to stop our spouse from expressing something to us because it hurts our ego. There are several benefits of listening to your partner:

- *You may learn something new about your partner*
- *You find out what's important to them*
- *You can be the person they will go to with anything*
- *Deeper understanding and trust*

With some couples, one partner will feel they can do no wrong. They constantly blame the other and do not listen when the other partner's needs are being openly expressed. How can a conflict be resolved if one party is not listening? Spoiler alert, it can't! It takes two to tango in this relationship, and both partners need to constantly work on the relationship.

For example: *Say you want to talk to your spouse about the chores around the house. You work part-time while your spouse works full time. You tell them how you are feeling, but before you can fully express how you are feeling, your partner cuts you off and says, "I am away at work all day so there's only so much I can do. I don't want to have this fight again." You decide to give up the argument, as you know your spouse will not bother to do any chores.*

This is not productive at all! We want to have open communication with each other. If you or your spouse cut each other off without listening, then conflicts will never be resolved. A huge part of listening is empathy. Learning to empathize with our partner's feelings is the main path to compromise.

Something else to keep in mind is that a listening ear may be all our partner's need! Have you ever just needed to vent? Maybe you had a terrible day and just need someone to listen. That's what our partner is for. They are supposed to be our best friends and always in our corner. We don't always need their advice or need them to fix things, but we just want them to support us by being attentive. While you may have strayed away from this a bit in your marriage, this is always something you can work on and get back to.

Express Openly

Express what you are feeling and need to change clearly! You and your partner cannot read each other's minds (sadly) so you have to be sure that your message is clear. Be specific about exactly what is bothering you and want you would like to see change. Lay it out for them! Don't leave any room for guessing, because this only opens up the possibility for more miscommunication.

For example: *Your partner tells you they are unhappy with the pickup schedule for the kids. You ask them if they want to change pick-up days or figure out a new schedule. They shrug and complain, saying they just have to do everything and are tired of carrying all the weight in the relationship.*

This is a simple example of someone not being clear! Do you know what they meant? How are they carrying all the weight in the relationship? I certainly don't know! What happens often in a marriage is one person will be able to openly express themselves while another struggles with this. Sometimes you may have to go a step farther and ask the right questions to get a direct answer: *What is upsetting you? Why does it upset you? How can I make you feel better? What can we do to change this right now?*

Note Body Language

As we talked in Chapter 1, 55% of all communication is body language. This is all nonverbal. Before we even speak, we are already communicating something to our partner. Much like the tone of voice, body language is something you and your partner will understand well about each other and may notice something is wrong before communicating through a speech about the issue. Can you and your partner communicate just by a look or a head nod? This is so great! But, it can also be a giveaway when one partner is upset.

When implementing your listening skills, direct eye contact is a substantial form of body language used to show your partner that you care, are engaged with what they are saying, and are going to continue to listen. Just like tone of voice, your body language can say something completely different from what you are verbally expressing. Make sure you are aware of how your body language comes off to your partner.

Good Timing

There is a time and place for everything! Choosing the right time to discuss with your partner will make communication easier. Picking a welcoming environment was one of our tips in the beginning of the chapter. This is good to be aware of so we can interpret what state of mind our partner is in.

Is your partner having a bad day? Do you know they have something important in the morning? Or, are you somewhere public where other people could overhear your discussion? The environment in which you discussed something has a huge effect on the outcome of the discussion.

For example: *You want to discuss your partner's spending. But, you know they have a work meeting early in the morning that they have spent the entire week preparing for. Early in the evening, they even expressed to you how nervous they are about it. They don't want to mess up and have been worrying about it for days. You decide to put off the conversation for another night when they are less stressed and can't focus on communicating with you.*

The respectful thing to do in this situation would be to wait until the next evening or until a few days have passed to talk to your partner about their spending. It can't hurt to wait a day, and they will be in a much better mindset to talk! Once the stressful work event is over, they will be ready to take other stressors on. But at the moment, that is the only stressor they can focus on.

They may feel attacked if you add more stress the evening before an already stressful event.

Important conversations also should not be put off for long periods. You want to be sure you aren't avoiding discussing core conflicts within your marriage. *Have you ever walked away from an argument feeling disappointed, angry, or like you didn't say all you wanted to?*

To avoid this, we want to really set aside time for our partners to ensure we give the attention that is needed to a situation. We will talk about the importance of time later in this chapter.

Trust

Trust is something that is built. But an effective marriage cannot function without it. If you have entered a sacred bond with your partner, then you trusted them at some point. Hopefully, you still do, but if you don't, there are ways you can get that trust back!

Trust means that you believe what your partner says and communicates to you. Think about all the things you must trust your partner with! Maybe finances, kids, home-owning, emotions, and more. Your marriage is a partnership. Leaning into this trust and recognizing it can help you grow closer to your partner. Trust cannot function without:

1. Honesty
2. Openness
3. Transparency

These things are other principles that we are learning to work on. The interesting thing about these principles is that many go hand in hand with the others. In marriage, our partner should be our "go-to" person! We want to believe in them and trust them with our struggles, worries, and everything else in our lives!

When there is trust in our marriage, it becomes a source of

constant *comfort* and *safety*. People don't trust their partners for a variety of reasons, but some may be as follows: *bad experience, afraid to trust, inconsistencies in the relationship.* These are all issues that need to be healed and discussed openly with your partner. They each form a core conflict.

Honesty

What is the point of having a partnership if you will not be honest? And how can you build trust without doing so? Be more honest in your marriage. Acknowledge these conflicts you are having! Many times, partners will not even do this. It can be out of fear that saying it aloud will make it real. Decide to put it all out there! Ask for the things you want and verbalize the things you like about your partner. There are several types of honesty within a marriage:

1. *Financial:* Being open about money, spending, expenses, etc.
2. *Media (Online):* Not hiding messages or social media profiles
3. *Emotional*: True expression of feelings, both positive & negative
4. *Physical*: Intimacy, expression of the need for more or less, PDA, etc.

Hiding anything at all in a marriage can have devastating results. Dishonesty will only lead to further miscommunication and mistrust. If you are dishonest about anything in your marriage, ask yourself why this might be. *Are you hiding things out of fear of judgment? Do you want to protect your partner from something?*

Whatever the reason is, you need to understand it. We will do more work on the individual self within your marriage in

Chapter 5, where we talk about what you specifically can do to improve your relationship.

Embody Gratitude

Throughout this entire process, we can get lost in trying to "fix" things. But, we have already built something great! Remember what drew you to your partner. Write their attributes, physical and emotional, that you like about them! There are so many things about all of us as people. You don't want to forget about these qualities of your partner.

Studies have shown that gratitude benefits both the person cultivating the gratitude and the person who is receiving that gratitude. So, if you and your partner are both feeling grateful for each other, then everyone wins! If only it were this easy!

Try to think about big and little things that you like about your partner. *Do they make you laugh when you need it? Are they empathetic to your feelings? Do they know how to handle the finances? Are they good with the kids?* There are endless aspects of your relationship and the qualities of your partner to be grateful for if you just inspect it.

No Comparing

Never forget that your relationship and marriage are unique to you and your partner. While you can look at other people around you and assume things, you will never know the truth about their relationship because you are not in it! Trust me, they too are struggling with core conflicts that are manifesting in ways you will never see. No marriage is perfect. Avoiding comparison to all aspects of life will lead you to a healthier lifestyle. Just because one couple is doing something does not mean you have to do it!

Hopefully, this guide has brought you some relief! You have a plan now! These things are crucial to a healthy marriage and proper communication with your partner. You will strengthen your trust and see that solving future issues will come much easier.

If you are still feeling uncertain about how to implement this into your marriage, the next chapter will be real-life examples that you can insert yourself into to see how you would react. Throughout this process, remember to be grateful for your spouse. While all the issues you and your partner will argue about are important, keep in mind that time is important as well. Our marriage adds quality to our lives and we need to nourish it to keep it alive and thriving.

Time as a Commodity

We can't stop time from passing. We only get so much in this life, and we don't want to waste any of it. If you are reading this, you have probably noticed on some level that you are wasting time fighting and miscommunicating with your partner. These principles will help you stop this habit and learn to cherish your time instead. Spending quality time with your spouse is just as important as following this guide. Many of these steps include spending time with one another. When we get used to our routine with our partner, we can forget to be present!

Does it ever feel like there is just not enough time in the day? Are you going to work then the gym, taking care of kids and chores? Life can be stressful and overwhelming. But the relationship you have built with your spouse is a precious and important one. If it is not nurtured and looked after, it will suffer. Truly acknowledging its delicacy will help you look at it from the right perspective.

Unfortunately, so many of us go about our minutes, hours, and days without realizing we now have one less minute, hour, and day! You and your partner chose each other for a reason, and you want to enjoy the time you have with each other. While I don't mean to scare you here! I only mean to bring a bit of perspective. We can get so caught up in the day-to-day issues, with our spouse and even in our own daily life, that we do not see what's right in front of us until it is too late.

Spending time together as a couple will help to strengthen your bond and naturally your communication as well. Doing things together will also help you find more things in common! Even just going grocery shopping together or doing chores with each other can make them more enjoyable. Love is in the little things. Maybe you want to take a weekend yoga or exercise class together. It does not matter what you choose to do, but that you choose to do it. Love and how you treat it is a choice. This entire process is a choice! And it's one you must make for the health of your marriage.

Equally important in this scenario is following through. If you tell your spouse that you will do something with them, then do it! There can be even less bonding if you commit to doing an activity with your spouse, then back out for whatever reason. This doesn't make anyone feel good in the situation, and it definitely will not bring the two of you together. It will create a bigger lapse in communication and a breakdown in honesty and trust.

Every couple is different and will need to spend more or less time together. This is another good opportunity to use the above guide to communicate and figure out what will work for both of you. You want to be sure you agree! Don't be afraid to ask how your partner feels about spending their time. *Do they feel the two of you spend enough time together? Would they like to try new things together?* These are questions that will help clarify where they stand for you and will help your partner to feel you are engaged and open in the relationship.

Setting Healthy Boundaries

Building communication and trust should be of the utmost importance for your marriage. Also at the top of your list should be healthy boundaries! You may think, *wait what? Aren't we working on building a greater connection in my marriage in this book?* And the answer to your question is yes! Of course, we are looking to do that. But, a huge part of that is knowing the difference between healthy and unhealthy boundaries. Like we talked about, our marriage is ano*ther* thing to us. It should brighten our life, lift us up, and make us feel good! But, it should not make us feel whole. We are still entitled to all the healthy boundaries along with everyone else, and just because we have entered into a partnership, it does not mean that these boundaries go away.

Healthy boundaries and the separation of self are at the foundation of a healthy marriage. These boundaries should be prioritized more so in a marriage, as they can become blurry. There are many kinds of boundaries within a marriage. We are going to define five primary types that are important to not only identify but properly understand before we can learn how to implement them in our communication with our partner. We will also look at some phrases and fill-in-the-blank exercises you can use if needed for each boundary.

1. Physical Boundaries

This type of boundary refers to your body, physical space, and privacy. Some people enjoy public displays of affection and some are uncomfortable with it. That's okay! You should not have to explain to your partner about things that make you uncomfortable. They are there to support you. But it's good to know how your partner feels either way.

There are also things your partner may want sexually that you may not be okay with. No one should pressure you into anything. Being married is no excuse. If you are uncomfortable with something, that is the end of the discussion! You need to assert yourself in boundary situations so it is clear to your partner what you are okay with and what you are not okay with.

This is where the communication portion comes in. Here are some phrases you can use when dealing with physical boundaries. Note that these phrases are "I statements" which is the first principle for communication.

I don't like it when you touch me in _____ way.
It makes me feel overwhelmed when you are always _____ near me.
I don't like public displays of affection because it makes me feel uncomfortable.

These statements are justified and good for boundary setting. You can even write out some things that are bothering you and reflect on them to figure out why they upset you. While you don't need to justify to your partner why something makes you uncomfortable, it can be good for your personal growth to understand why a certain physical action brings you uncomfortable feelings.

2. Emotional Boundaries

Relying on our partner is a good thing, but we need to handle our own emotions too. Recognizing our feelings is where healthy boundaries begin. Having the awareness to notice when you are feeling sad, angry, happy, guilty can be helpful to communicate them properly to your partner.

This is another area where we can write things down to understand them. Journaling is a great tactic to chart our emotions. We can see day to day what is upsetting us or making us happy or angry, etc. Then, once we understand the situations that are causing the emotion, we can communicate it to our partner. Try using some of the following statements:

I felt _____ *when you said/did* _____.
It made me feel _____ *when we were talking about* _____.

While these may seem like simple exercises/communication tools, they can make all the difference when discussing difficult topics. People will often avoid talking and enforcing their boundaries within their marriage out of fear that their partner will reject them.

Emotionally, we want our partner to accept us. But holding things in can be damaging. This will only make the relationship more unhealthy, as the long-term effects of unhealthy boundaries can be damaging.

3. Financial Boundaries

All about the money! As we talked about in the previous chapter, money can be a core conflict. It is a tremendous source of stress and especially within a relationship. Some couples need joint or separate bank accounts to manage their money. You and your partner should use the 10-Principle guide to discuss the best course of action for you. No couple will be the same!

Some will have more discretion within their spending and some will have less. Some people are also better with money than others. I know some couples where one partner manages all the money, and the other is happy with that! It all depends. There is no right or wrong way, as long as you communicate and agree with one another.

I want to go _____ *with you but we both need to contribute.*

I really think we need a new _____ can we budget for it?

Note that these are still "I statements." Aren't these great? When stated honestly and with an even tone of voice, statements are one of the most useful tools for communication, especially about sensitive topics. Money stresses everyone out! It is a necessary part of our lives, and when we are married, we have to work on it together.

4. Intellectual Boundaries

This type of boundary includes your ideas and beliefs. A healthy boundary is when both partners are respectful of the original ideas of the other. Many partners see things differently. Maybe you even believe different things too!

Some couples have one religious partner and one who is not. Whatever it is, we want to be sure we are not talking down to our partners or putting down anything that they are passionate about. When we are married, it means we accept our partners for everything, including their values and intellect. If you feel you can't discuss something with your partner out of fear of judgment, then a boundary needs to be put in place.

I feel _____ when you put down my faith.
It hurts me when you call my ideas stupid.
I support your _____ but you do not support me.

A lack of support in your marriage can lead to mistrust and damage your connection. As stated, our partner should be our "go to" person! They are the ones who we should be able to talk to and know will support us through anything. Sadly, things will not always be this way. But, it doesn't mean you can't get it back! It can be a simple boundary issue that needs to be addressed.

Sometimes, there can also be a deeper issue of basic rights not being respected, which we will talk about in the next section.

Your Basic Rights

As humans, we all have basic rights. This is not up for discussion, and we do not need to explain ourselves when asserting these. If we notice these rights are not being respected, this is absolutely a time to set a boundary. Within a relationship, these basic rights are still in place, but there may be additional expectations and rights within the relationship. If you are feeling confused or unsure on exactly what basic rights you have, especially within your relationship, here are a few examples:

1. Saying No

Within your relationship, you may say no. Whether this is to go out to dinner, or during intimacy, you can set this boundary for yourself. We all know when something another person is asking of us may be against our wishes, values, or needs. This is the time to assert yourself. And the best part about this is that you should not have to defend yourself!

It's difficult to say no to our partners, as we might not want to upset them or hurt their feelings. But you know when something isn't right for you! And, your partner should want the best for you and always respect what you express to them. Know that this is a basic right in all areas of your life.

2. Ask Questions

This is crucial for communication. If you feel you cannot ask questions in your marriage because of upsetting your partner, then something is wrong. This needs to be communicated and respected immediately. You may ask questions about everything, such as finances, friendships, and your partner's whereabouts when they are not showing up where they should be. If they make you feel bad for asking simple questions, this needs to be communicated. You may ask! You are their husband/wife, after all.

3. Form Outside Relationships

It is completely healthy to have outside relationships with other people. We all have family and friends who we are close to! If you feel that you cannot have these outside relationships, for whatever reason, then this is a right that is being violated within your relationship. You and your partner should be able to rely on one another, but you should not be the only people you communicate with and spend your time with.

4. Make Mistakes

We are imperfect beings! We will make mistakes. Now, these mistakes do not extend to things such as abuse or infidelity, but minor mistakes should be forgiven. You are in a trusting partnership and your partner should not chastise you for small things we all do from time to time. Humans make mistakes, and we all show up late now and again, forget to do the dishes, vacuum, etc. There are countless minor mistakes we make. Our partner has loved us despite these flaws. We should not be berated every time we make a slight mistake.

5. Ask For Help

As stated before, our partner is our "go to" person. Everyone needs help. We cannot do everything alone. Our marriage is there to lift us and guide us when we need it the most. We will need help with big and small things. Your partner is now your family, and family always comes first! *What happens when we need someone to be there for us if we feel sick? What about if we break a bone?* These are important questions to ask, as this is the person you will be with for the rest of your life.

6. Love & Be Loved

You are married to your partner because you love them and they love you! Asking to feel loved is not too much. These were part of your vows, promising to love one another. You may love them and expect the same in return.

7. Feel Safe

Feel emotionally, mentally, and physically safe within your marriage. If you do not, then there may be abuse going on, and reach out to friends and family for help. When these rights are continuously ignored, and even after you implement the principle guide, yet your partner does not seem to pay any regard, it may be time to leave. An abusive relationship can be physical, emotional, and mental.

An abusive relationship can include any of one or a combination of the following: your partner constantly berates you, puts you down, yells and screams at you, or goes so far to physically hit you. They may even use psychological tactics such as gaslighting or use projection.

Gaslighting is used to manipulate someone into questioning their sanity and projection is when your partner will accuse you of things they are doing. These are damaging to the psyche.

These rights should not only be respected in your relationship but prioritized! They are the foundation to a healthy and successful marriage. If any of these are being continuously disrespected regularly, then it may be time for a more serious change.

Be Positive & Imagine Success

Throughout this journey, remember to stay positive! While this is certainly a cliche phrase, it's also true. Nothing good can come from being negative. There is a strong correlation between positivity and health. Surely you are looking to improve the overall positivity in your marriage. And to do that, we need that positive perspective!

You can also work on the things you imagine for you and your partner. *Do you see the best outcome in the future? Do you set aside time to daydream about the perfect relationship?* Surely this may sound silly, but it's also true!

There are many names for this, such as the law of attraction, manifesting, etc. In the end, you want to assume the best outcome. Nothing bad can come out of this. If you expect the best for you and your partner, then you will strive for it!

The benefits to staying positive are endless:

- increased resilience
- decreased stress/anxiety
- increased gratitude
- increased self-esteem
- emotional regulation
- improvement in sleep
- increased lifespan
- increased productivity

There are many more reasons, but as you can see, there are no downsides to being positive. While you are doing so, remember to enjoy this process as well. You are doing the steps to get where you and your partner want to be in your marriage. No one is perfect, and we all have flaws that can be worked on. While these principles are not set in stone, they can guide you to be more attentive to your partner's needs and concerns.

Chapter Summary

- Tips for conflict
- STRENGTHEN 10-Principle Guide
- Time as a Commodity & Staying Positive

In the next chapter, you will learn examples for each principle and how to use them effectively.

4

REAL LIFE EXAMPLES & SOLUTIONS

Now that you are prepared with your **STRENGTHEN 10-Principle Guide**, we can put these into action! These steps can seem intimidating and you may wonder how it is you are supposed to use this in your marriage. This chapter will help you relate to real-life situations and understand how to incorporate them into your marriage.

We will go through each principle again, and use examples of how they can be effective and how not using them will cause a deeper conflict! Try to imagine yourself and your spouse in these situations. Think of how you normally would react and think of how you would react after using the principles. These examples will be relatable to you, as they will embody different versions of core conflicts. Each example can be transferred into your situation.

After each sample, there will be a section after each example called *what would you do?* This is the time to reflect on how you would react to the situation. Write it down if you'd like, and understand why you would react this way. Writing it down may be useful as you can keep track of your immediate response, and then the response you would like to see after implementing the principle.

Example #1: Statements

Mia is tired of her husband not listening to her emotional needs. She feels that he no longer wants to spend time together. She asks almost every night that they watch a movie together, but he says he would prefer to watch his show on Netflix. She has never told him why she wants to spend time with him. It is because she feels a lack of connection in their relationship.

Another night, she asks him to watch a movie, and he says no. She screams at him, "You don't care about me or this relationship! Why are we even together?" Her husband is confused and taken back by her yelling, as he didn't realize that she was so upset by him not watching a movie with her. Meanwhile, she is still frustrated and feeling an overall lack of connection.

This is a great example of how not only communication is important, but the way we state our feelings is important too. Mia blew up on her husband! She let the way she was feeling simmer, and instead of telling him she wanted to spend time with him, she let him continue to say no.

While she may have had a right to get upset, she did never really express to him why she was feeling the way she was. Then when she blew up over something that seemed small to her husband, she related it to the relationship.

We are not mind readers! If she had told her husband, this may have ended differently. And it may not have! But we can't assume anything for our partners. And, when she finally told her husband what was wrong, she did it with "you statements" vs. "I statements."

<u>What would you do?</u>

Think of how you would react better in this situation. Would you have blown up like this? Maybe in the past, and maybe you still might. This is okay. But we want to heighten our awareness so that we can try to keep this to a minimum. Using "I statements" is so helpful, and in Mia's case, should have been done way earlier!

In your marriage, don't let issues like this sit. The longer we let issues sit, the bigger they build up in our minds. Express to your partner why you want to spend time with them!

Don't assume they can read your mind, because although we can be extremely close to our partners, they can't possibly always know what we are thinking.

Example #2: Tone of Voice

John and Anne are arguing because Anne's mother is coming into town. John is a successful painter, but Anne's mother talks down to him because she doesn't think art is an actual profession. She makes him feel bad, and he doesn't like when she is around. He hates when she comes to visit, and Anne knows it.

Anne is trying to schedule plans for the weekend and a nice dinner for Saturday night. She is asking John if he would like to go to his favorite steak restaurant downtown. She suggests this to make her mother's visit more enjoyable for him. John responds in a high-pitched tone, saying, "I don't care what we do!" Anne can tell he is unhappy with her mother coming.

In-laws can cause lots of problems! This situation busts the myth that problems within a marriage cannot come from outside sources.

While Anne is not her mother, John is having a tough time separating the two. He does not want her to visit. Anne is trying her best to manage the situation by suggesting they go to his favorite restaurant, but his tone of voice gives him away.

Not only this, but he expresses to Anne that he does not care what they do. While this may not be true to his relationship with her, she certainly feels like it is aimed at her.

What would you do?

It's difficult to be empathetic, especially for our partner's family. But think of your relationship with your partner. The two of you are now family. How would you feel if someone on her side of the family did not like you and caught an attitude every time you were around? This would make things miserable. Try to keep this in mind when your in-laws are around next time.

Example #3: Really Listen!

Noah loves to play video games to destress from his corporate job. His wife, Violet, thinks this is silly. She hates that he does this and feels that he can't focus on anything else when he plays video games. They have three children together, and once a week Noah has to pick them up from school because Violet works late that day.

She reminds him he has to get the kids extra early on his pickup day that week because their youngest daughter has a doctor's appointment. He is playing video games when she tells him, and he nods but doesn't hear her. When the pickup day comes, he is late, and their youngest daughter misses her appointment.

A few things are going on in this scenario, as they're usually in miscommunication situations! Noah wasn't listening when his wife expressed what needed to be done for their younger daughter. But, she also chose the worst time to tell him, knowing that he does not listen well when he is playing video games.

Both partners in this scenario need to change their behavior. Violet needs to more openly express her feelings about when he plays video games.

While it is enjoyable for Noah, there could be set times for him to do so, and this way, there wouldn't be a lapse in communication. It's important for him to still play, as it is part of himself, but it should not consume all his time.

What would you do?

Certainly in every marriage, there are things your partner does that drive you crazy! But, being aware of these things and when to express them can make a vast difference. How would you express to your partner that they need to really listen in this scenario?

Try picking a time when they are not engaging in those activities that you know drive you crazy because they know you know they will not be listening! Phew! What a mouthful! But it's true. This way, you will avoid all the assumptions and communicate directly.

Example #4: Express Openly

Oliver has been acting strange towards his wife. She asks him if something is wrong. He says that he is feeling frustrated with her. She asks him why, and he tells her to forget it and that it's not worth arguing about. But the rest of the day, he acts standoffish towards her. She wants to ask him again but decides not to avoid an argument.

This is an example of a couple expressing openly with each other. Oliver could simply tell his wife what he is feeling, but he holds it in. That is his choice to do so, but then he cannot hold it over her head, especially when she doesn't even know what she has done wrong! His wife also stops asking about what the problem is, and we see a lack of communication from both partners. They are both holding back now, and it will eventually bubble up to the surface over something else.

What would you do?

In this situation, it's best to communicate directly with your partner. Holding something over their head that they don't even understand is unfair and can even become manipulative. We want to express openly, using the principles beforehand (tone of voice, "I statements," really listening) to express our genuine emotions.

Example #5: Note Body Language

Abigail has noticed that the dishwasher at her house does not work as well as she thought. She talks to her husband, James, about maybe getting a new one. Their finances have been tight lately, so she was dreading bringing it up. She says, "We need a new dishwasher, what do you think?" he says, "Yeah, great idea." But, when he says this, he rolls his eyes and lifts his eyebrows. Abigail decides to not order the washer because she can tell that her husband does not want to order it.

James's body language is saying something completely different from what he is expressing verbally. He is not interested in getting that washer! But, he says it is a great idea. Abigail can easily pick up on him, not wanting to spend money on the washer. While the couple is communicating nonverbally, it is not effective communication. Both are left feeling upset and unsatisfied by the interaction.

What would you do?

We want to be aware of our body language and how our words may conflict with it. Our inner feelings will show through our body language whether we want them to! Our partners are often the closest to us, and they will catch onto this. Try to cultivate an awareness of this. Consciously think not only about the words you say but about how your body is reacting to your true inner feelings.

Example #6: Good Timing

Jake and his wife, Nora, are out to dinner with another couple they are friends with. Jake is drinking a lot. He is slurring his words, and Nora feels embarrassed. She has noticed he has been drinking more. She thinks about saying something to him at the moment but decides not to. She instead makes an excuse and tells the other couple she has a severe headache and drives him home.

Nora made an excellent choice in this scenario! Her husband would not have been in the right state of mind to discuss anything, even if she had tried to. It also may have been embarrassing for both her and him if she brought up his drinking in front of their friends. Jake was not even in the right state of mind to have a discussion, regardless of where they were. He was completely intoxicated. The communication was already compromised just by his state of being.

What would you do?

Have you ever been in a situation like this with your partner? Maybe not necessarily when they were drunk, but maybe they were doing something that was embarrassing you? The best thing to do would be to wait until you are both alone and then discuss with your partner what is bothering you. This is more respectful to you and them. It's not so much about being secretive, but certain things should be kept within a marriage.

Exercise #7: Trust

Jack has been having a lot of negative feelings lately. He thinks it may be anxiety. He got a promotion at work, which he should have felt good about, but he's finding the change extremely stressful. His wife, Hannah, threw him a surprise party and invited all his friends over to congratulate him. He is worried about telling her his genuine feelings about the promotion, but he knows she loves and cares for him.

One evening after dinner, he tells her he needs to talk to her. When he explains his feelings, she hugs him and tells him she completely understands.

She then goes even further to help him find a therapist who specializes in anxiety.

This is a great example of a trusting relationship. While Jack didn't want to let his wife down, he knew he could trust in her. She is his "go to" person! Not only this, but she knew she could only help him so much and even helped him look for a professional to further discuss his feelings with.

Both partners in this situation are trusting and honest. Hannah could have been upset and said that she threw an entire party for him, only for him to express his genuine feelings about the promotion. But she reacts healthily and completely understands. Jack also tells her at an appropriate time. He does not tell her at the surprise party, as this would not have been the environment to do so.

<u>What would you do?</u>

Have you ever really needed to talk to your partner, but you've held back? Think about what this reason is. If it's out of fear or judgment or you feel they don't listen to you, this is something you need to communicate with them. Using "I statements" you can tell them how you feel you cannot express openly with them. You can explain that this lack of openness will only lead to a lack of trust.

Exercise #8: Honesty

* Trust and honesty often go hand in hand, so I will use the same couple from the above exercise for this principle *

Hannah has been noticing that Jack is extremely stressed. She doesn't know why because things have been going well for him. He just received a promotion at work and will make substantially more money. She asks him what's wrong. He snaps at her and says that nothing is wrong. Jack decides not to tell Hannah because he is ashamed to be stressed about his new position. She can tell something is wrong and wonders why he won't tell her.

In this example, the couple's trust is diminishing. Jack was not honest with her, and Hannah knows this. In a marriage, our spouses know us well! We have talked about this many times, how our partners will pick up on behavior in more ways than we realize. By not telling her, he is making the situation worse for both of them. Hannah can tell he is being dishonest, and this places unnecessary strain on their relationship.

What would you do?

Are there things that you are not honest with your partner about? If so, why? We are all individuals and should have private lives to a degree, but we shouldn't be dishonest with our partners either. Before keeping anything to yourself, think of how it will look to your partner. Will it appear secretive or deceitful? If so, honesty would be better.

Exercise #9: Embody Gratitude

Lily and Sam have been arguing lately. They are behind on bills and stress levels are high. Their 10th wedding anniversary is coming up, and Lily doesn't know what to get Sam, as they are budgeting tight. However, Lily is a talented painter, and she paints their wedding photo for him. When she gives him the present, he cries and can feel how much she cares for him.

For expressing our feelings, it can be in the little things. These meaningful expressions of love can mean more than fancy, expensive gifts. Lily took the time to paint something that showed the love shared between her and Sam.

What would you do?

We can get so wrapped up in day-to-day things that we forget the beautiful bond we share with our partner. We are lucky to have this person! They love us and want to be with us. Can you think of a time when your partner showed they were grateful for you or you did this for them? How did you feel? This is important to keep in mind so we don't lose sight of what is important in our lives.

Exercise #10: No Comparing

Addison and David are friends with two couples from David's golf club. Whenever they are together, the other couples are always touching each other and kissing. Addison and David rarely engage in PDA because it makes Addison uncomfortable. However, Addison doubts herself and wonders if she and David are not as close as the other couples. At home, she asks him what he thinks about the PDA. He kisses her and says, "I think we are just fine the way we are."

In this situation, Addison doubts her feelings because of what she sees other couples doing. Though she knows she doesn't like PDA, once she sees other couples kissing, she doubts herself. But, everyone is different! Her husband then reassures her, telling her they are fine the way they are. This example also shows that she and David have a strong relationship because she trusts him enough to tell him her feelings about the PDA.

<u>*What would you do?*</u>

As humans, it's natural to compare. Many times, it's not out of malicious intent, but out of a general curiosity of how we could be better. Couples keep most of their problems to themselves. You will not always see other couples fighting or see the petty arguments that go on over laundry, finances, etc. Don't compare your worst moments with your partner to their best moments!

. . .

While these are only fictional examples, I'm sure you will find many of these relatable! I sure did! As we saw in Chapter Three, all couples face those core conflicts but they just take different forms! Using these principles, we can overcome them. If you're still feeling alone in the issues you and your partner suffer, we are going to look at some facts about marriage, like why people get married, divorced, etc.

Fast Facts About Marriage

Looking at some facts about marriage is a useful tool to know that you are not alone. While statistics do not apply to everyone, it is a great way to see that other people also struggle within their relationship! All marriages are different, and not all will fall into the following statistics. These statistics are just to help show you that many people suffer from the same kinds of conflicts and that by following the principles in this book, you can work towards a healthier marriage and partnership with your spouse. You want to avoid becoming another statistic!

According to the Pew Research Center, there are several major reasons people get married. The following are listed in order of importance:

1. Love
2. Making a lifelong commitment
3. Companionship
4. Having children
5. A relationship that is recognized through a religious ceremony
6. Financial stability
7. Legal rights and benefits

It's interesting that the top two reasons are love and making a lifelong commitment. I believe this just shows even more so that people are looking for their "go to" person in life! They are not so much worried about financial stability or their legal rights, which is quite interesting. People would rather have their person in life. Think of this within your relationship. What would you say is the most important reason for being together? There is no wrong answer. Every couple comes together for different reasons, but hopefully, the foundation is love and care for one another.

This study shows how much we value connection! Therefore, it is so crucial to rebuilding that connection within your marriage! With a stronger connection comes stronger trust and a better marriage. If love and a lifelong commitment are the most important reason people get married, then it is probably safe to assume they are at least some of the top reasons people stay together as well! Pew Research also found three important reasons for staying married:

- Having shared interests
- Satisfying sexual relationship
- Sharing household chores

* Note that these reasons can be maintained through effective communication! *

Having shared interests can be worked on through many of our principles. We also talked about in the previous chapter how time is a commodity. Shared interests are a way that people spend time together. Noting that this is one of the major reasons people stay married can help you put your mind in the right place. It will also help you know where to start! How can a marriage work if you are not spending time together? We want to be with our partners and feel that connection. Shared interests are a way to feel this connection.

A satisfying sexual relationship happens through none other

than communication. When is the last time you and your partner talked about sex? Don't let yourselves fall into the trap of getting too comfortable and assuming you're both happy. This is how miscommunication happens. Sex is important for people because we are social creatures. While the spectrum is different for each person, and some will need it more than others, humans thrive on close personal relationships.

The third reason for staying married, household chores, is interesting. Household chores are such a tiny problem if you think about it. In the grand scheme of life, they mean nothing! I don't think anyone, at the end of their life, says, "Wow, I wish I vacuumed more." This is just not something I have encountered yet. But maybe they do! These pesky household chores can be communicated about and tackled together. However, they may show something deeper. We may hold a deeper issue inside of us and instead of sharing, we hold it, creating tension. Then, when we least expect it, it bubbles up. This could be over something like household chores.

Not only can these be maintained through effective communication, but they can be improved upon by using the STRENGTHEN 10-Principle Guide. Having shared interests may not be something you and your partner share right now, but it can be! You can cultivate shared interests and find alternative ways to spend time together.

- A divorce happens every 36 seconds in the U.S.! This is roughly 876,000 divorces per year.
- One in seven married people has contemplated divorce because of their partner's social media activity. (This statistic ties into the need for online media honesty!)
- Online affairs cause one in three divorces.
- Around 6% of American couples marry, divorce, and then remarry each other.

What!! This last fact blew my mind. 6% is many people. What is the point of divorcing only to remarry when you can solve a good number of problems through proper communication? Of course, this is not for all couples. Some couples rightfully separate for reasons that are personal to them, and that is fine! They do not need to justify that to anyone. But, for the couples who split due to core conflicts, they need the STRENGTHEN Guide! If we can prevent divorce by using these communication principles to get to the core conflict, then we absolutely should!

Online and social media activity causes a lot of issues. It is a different time than we live in now. Everything is available online, to where it is almost scary. We have to trust our partner in alternative ways rather than just in person. They may chat with or follow people online that we are not familiar with. One in seven people is a shockingly high number. And these people are contemplating divorce solely because of their partner's online activity. This is something that needs to be communicated and sorted out immediately

These facts are not meant to scare you! They correlate with much of what we have been speaking about. These core conflicts play a role in how partners consider divorce. We see social media and online activity causing issues. This is all a part of trust and honesty within the relationship. Without effective communication, we cannot expect our relationship to have any problems!

Can I Save the Marriage by Myself?

What a great question. Thank you for asking! Basically, no. But don't be discouraged! Often when our spouse sees us putting in more work, they naturally do the same. Our partners love us, and they too want the best for the marriage deep down. While it's true that we can't be the only ones to put in the work for the marriage, we certainly can promote a positive change through our own behavior.

If the marriage only involved one person, then the answer would be yes, you could save it. But it takes two to tango, as I've stated many times. But just because it takes two doesn't mean that the one spouse working hard to save the marriage should give up. It's admirable to be putting in all this work. You may read this book alone, wondering why even bother doing so, especially if your spouse doesn't care as much as you do. But, who's to say they don't? From now on, you can use the communication tools in your **STRENGTHEN 10-Principle** Guide to talk to them and find out where their mindset is.

In the meantime, let's talk about some things that don't work and that do work when trying to work on your marriage. This way, you can know what to expect as you talk with your spouse and try to gauge their reaction. Here are some actions that will not work:

1. Forcing Your Spouse to Stay

This is not good. We don't want to be in any kind of relationship. Who doesn't want to be in a relationship with us, right? That is a miserable way to live. You deserve better and so do they! Remember that. Also, we cannot force anyone to do anything. Everyone is their person. We each make our own choices in life. If someone wants to leave, then they may do so.

2. Manipulating Your Spouse

Using money, children, or blackmail to get your spouse to stay is a huge no. It is also extremely abusive. There's no need to do this, and you should not treat someone that you care about this way. Try to keep in mind how you would like to be treated by your spouse and treat them the same way from now on. How would you feel about them playing mind games? You probably would not like this, rightfully so. Do not treat them so you would not want to be treated.

3. Making Them Jealous

This is an extremely toxic and unhealthy way to communicate. While it's communication, I'll give you that, it's manipulation and indirect communication. It will do nothing but drive a bigger wedge between you and your spouse. Why would you want to make them feel bad? You are trying to build a connection with them! Not create a bigger separation.

Acting Desperate

It's good to show our spouse that we are serious about saving the marriage. But we do not want to act desperate and follow them around, forsaking ourselves. This will cause us to appear less attractive, as we will fade far away from the person we were when we were first married. What will work when trying to save your marriage is getting back to what first attracted your partner to you in the beginning?

Normally, four primary things cause attraction to another person. They are physical, emotional, intellectual, and spiritual attractions. You must have had some of these attributes for your partner to be attracted to you! And you may have noticed one or multiple of these things about your partner initially. Embodying each of these attractions in your way can work to help your marriage. Let's talk about each type of attraction and how you can use this to work on your marriage.

Physical

Everyone is attracted to different physical attributes. Think of what you looked like when you were first married. While we don't want to change ourselves too much, let's remember this initial attraction and try to tap into this as much as possible. Maybe you used to wear certain clothes that your partner found unique, or you took good care of your physical health through exercising and eating well. We can get back to this by implementing healthier habits. If our physical attraction has decreased for whatever reason, we can get it back with some hard work.

Emotional

Are you funny? Or super sensitive to your partner's feelings? Do you still embody this emotional attractiveness to them? Or have you swayed from this a bit?

Think of ways that you might get back to it! It may be a simpler fix than you think. You can always start telling jokes again or asking about their day in the way you used to.

Spiritual

Did you have values at the beginning of the relationship that you don't have now? Maybe you didn't drink before, but now you do. This is all okay, but try to figure out what changed, and how you might get back to it.

Maybe you and your partner met at church, but life got in the way and you both don't go anymore. Try to invite them to go with you. Connected spiritually with your partner can help lead the path for you to reconnect in other ways.

Intellectual

Everyone loves a good conversation. Maybe you and your partner used to talk for hours, and now you barely even see each other. Or, maybe you are extra smart and used to discuss topics your spouse was interested in. Now, you don't do this too much anymore.

Figure out why this is. Think about this! Then, try to spend time with your partner, and just talk to them. Ask them what they are thinking. A stimulating conversation may be what they are looking for from you. We can get so busy with our daily life that we forget to have important conversations with our partners.

After reading the real-life examples in this chapter, hopefully, you have been able to apply them to your marriage! There are so many ways to do this. And these facts certainly were eye-opening. It's crucial to know what is important for most people in a relationship. You can then compare this to yours and see if it correlates. If it does, great! If not, this is another opportunity to communicate with your partner and find the best solution for both of you.

Chapter Summary

- Exercises for each principle
- What would you do?
- Fast facts about marriage

In the next chapter, you will learn what you can do as an individual within your marriage.

5

SO WHAT CAN YOU DO?

We have discussed the Principles you can implement with your partner in your relationship. But, are there steps you can take individually to improve your marriage? The answer is yes! Absolutely.

This chapter is just as serious as Chapter 3, as we will talk about how to improve yourself, which is just as important as dealing with the core conflicts in your relationship. How can you expect the whole thing to work if one part isn't functioning properly? While I insinuate you are broken, I think we can all make improvements as a person. The stronger we are as individuals, the stronger our marriage will be together.

Sometimes, the best way to fix your marriage is by fixing yourself. Marriage is work! If there is anything you have learned so far in this journey, it should be that! It is a constant learning process and takes a great deal of patience. But, when you love someone and have built a life together, it's worth putting in the work!

Many people fall into the trap of "easing up" when they get

married. They think, *Well! All the hard work is done!* It's quite the opposite. Any relationship needs constant care and attention to stay healthy. We have to continue to take care of ourselves and find fresh ways to energize and uplift ourselves and the relationship. We want to keep spicing' it up!

When things are going wrong in our marriage, we usually will talk with close friends or family about our feelings and things that we would like to change. This is good and can be a big stress reliever for us, but most of the conversations will center on what our partner should change or do differently. *If only they would change, then everything would be better.* But what about us? Don't we play a role? We do. We play at least 50%.

Imagine how anything would be in your life if it was 50% better. What about your salary? What if that was 50% better? That's a vast difference! Taking responsibility for your role in the marriage right now will improve your marriage greatly. Often when our partners see us working on ourselves, they will respond.

How to Make the Relationship 50% Better

There are several tips I can give you that have worked for me and that I have seen in action in other marriages. These all connect with the idea that our marriage is an *Other* and without two healthy individual parts, we cannot expect to have a whole.

Decide to Change

Making the conscious choice to change sounds easier than it is. Just like our marriage, we can get comfortable with how we are. But life is constantly changing, and we have to adapt to new situations as they come.

Just because we want to change something about our lives, but that doesn't mean we are going to do it. There are several things we can change right now, such as:

1. Behavior

Are there things you do you know your spouse doesn't like? But, you still do it? Try to choose to stop and respect their wishes. We are usually too busy focusing on our spouse and things they do we don't like.

Try to turn that judgment inward and see things from their perspective. It can be something small at first, but noticing our behavior allows us to then change it.

2. Attitude

Maybe there are things you like and don't like about your spouse. Focusing on the good things can set you up for a better perspective. What are the things that first attracted you to them in the first place? Think of everything here. Their beauty, intellect, and emotion.

Retraining your mind to automatically focus on the positive is a great way to adjust your reaction to future conflict. You can do this by complimenting your spouse and thanking them for all they do within your marriage.

3. Heart

Get that heart in the right place! Put your partner's needs and wants before your own. Remember how much you care for them. You want the best for them, right? Try to remember this even in moments when you and your spouse may argue that your love for them is strong.

Challenge Yourself

If you have been married for a long time, you have probably settled into a comfortable routine and find a minor challenge in your daily life. Challenging ourselves is a great way to grow and improve. You learn to step outside your comfort zone and find alternative ways to solve problems. If you stop challenging yourself physically, mentally, spiritually, then there's nothing new to look forward to! You want to wake up every day to a challenge, to the excitement, and your life!

There are a million ways to challenge yourself, but some ideas are trying a new hobby, finally writing that book you've always wanted to, deciding to start a fitness routine, and more. You can bring a new skill set of problem-solving to your marriage when you learn to love a challenge.

Rid Yourself of the Stressors You Can

If there are certain stressors in the marriage that you can solve individually, do it. And do it now! The fewer problems you and your spouse have to worry about, the more you can focus on one another. For example, if you have financial stress, try to take care of this as soon as possible.

This is one of the core conflicts! And we often take our stress out on each other when really, it's not our partner's fault and we are in it together.

Stressors can add up before we realize it. Then, the stress of the relationship is just the cherry on top! In the worst-case scenario, it is the straw on the camel's back. And we do not want this! We want to eliminate the outside stressors so that we can focus all of our energy on the internal ones.

Educate Yourself

Take the time yourself to read about marriage techniques and better ways to communicate. For example, read this book! Exposing yourself to new ways of thinking, new ideas, and beliefs can broaden your perspective and help you see the conflicts within your marriage from the outside. When we are so close to something, it's difficult to see it. Bringing new information into your mind will produce new results outside of it.

Your Own Health in the Relationship

Prioritizing your health in a relationship is just as important as prioritizing the relationship itself. You need to be the best version of yourself before you can have the best version possible of your relationship!

So how can you become this *best version*? Working on yourself doesn't mean you have to follow anyone's particular rules or guidelines for changing.

Everything in this book is a tip! As I've stated, everything should be taken on your judgment. At the end of everything, only you know what is right for you and what truly aligns with your values and beliefs!

You don't want to change who you are deep down. You only want to make sure that you are as healthy as possible for this partnership.

So, on that note, let's get into a few tips about how to improve your overall health in the relationship. This includes physical, mental, emotional, spiritual. There may even be more! But, these are the basics. There are so many ways you can work on yourself in the relationship, but these are some ways you can do so today at this moment.

1. Spend Time Alone!

Yes, we have talked about how time is so important to spend with our partner. But time is a commodity for yourself too! Some people prefer to be alone more so than others.

You need to put the work and dedication into your own life and well-being. Spend time with you. Be your own best friend.

Learn the things that you like to do, don't like to do. If you need some time apart from your partner, take it! Doing so can bring you back together stronger than before. It is not personal to want alone time. We all need space to reset and get back to ourselves

2. Remember Your Friends

Our outside relationships are a crucial part of who we are. They are a basic right within the relationship. Spending time with other people reminds us of the other parts of ourselves and brings joy to our lives in ways we forget.

As you get more comfortable in your relationship, naturally be getting back to these other, outside relationships!

In a new marriage, we may still spend most of our time with our spouse, but as we get more comfortable, we can return to how things were before.

3. Hobbies

Most people have hobbies that their spouse does not. Some couples have things they like to do together and apart. I have friends who love to run, but their husbands don't. So they run together!

It's important to stay in touch with things that we are passionate about even while in a relationship with someone else. Tapping into these things keeps us in touch with who we are as a person so that we don't lose sight of the things we love. Maybe you don't feel you have hobbies right now. That's okay!

As we talked about in the previous section, we can always educate ourselves. It's never too late to learn a new skill or find a new passion!

4. Exercise

Equally important as having hobbies is exercise! When we exercise, endorphins are released, which are natural chemicals that are good for our health, and work to calm us down.

Exercise is a great stress reliever and improves our physical health as well. There are so many ways to get active, whether it be running outside, biking, weight lifting, exercise class, etc.

5. Goals

This is important to keep in mind if you're married! But especially in a marriage, it can become all-consuming and we forget the things we wanted to do before we entered this partnership. Marriage could be a goal for some people. But once you reach it, what is your next school?

Having consistent goals is a way to feel productive and a reason to wake up in the morning. It's also a way to separate yourself from the relationship. It's not so much that we need to separate ourselves, but recognizing that we are a person with goals that may differ from our partner is okay and healthy!

Try to keep all this in mind when thinking of your relationship. Becoming the best version of yourself does not have to be hard work. And it definitely should not be about changing who you are. It should instead be about tapping into those parts of you that may have been put on hold since you've entered this partnership.

Your partner fell in love with you! Remember this. We never want to get too far away from ourselves at any point in our life. During our marriage, we can sometimes forsake the things we once loved to do, and we can do it all the while thinking we are sacrificing for our marriage. But really, our marriage is suffering because of it. You know on airplanes when they tell you if anything happens, to put your mask on first before helping others. This is the same situation! It's time to work on your health and well-being before you can focus on marriage. This may appear selfish, but it is quite the opposite. We will talk about this in the next section.

Self-Love Within a Marriage Is Not Selfish

You may wonder how this chapter applies to your marriage. *Isn't it selfish to only care about what I'm doing and feeling in the marriage?* Of course, we do not want to only be thinking of ourselves, but working on our part of the marriage will only help the whole be stronger and better in the long run. Therefore, let's keep in mind:

How can you expect the marriage to feel strong and confident if you do not feel that way toward yourself? You want to be as solid as an individual as possible to make the marriage the same way. Of course, we are all human beings and will have our times of doubt, uncertainty, self consciousness, but overall, we want to be aware of who we are inside. So let's look at some reasons why you should incorporate self-love into your marriage.

The Way You Speak to Yourself Is How You Speak to Others

Have you ever heard of the Golden Rule: Treat others how you would like to be treated? Well, this is the flipped version of that. Your inner life can translate to your outer life as well. While we want to implement the golden rule and treat others how we want to be treated, the way we treat ourselves can be how we end up treating others.

Maybe we can call this one the Silver Rule? Maybe! Either way, it's good to remember to be kind to yourself. Your inner dialogue says a lot about you. We can be our harshest critics, and we hold ourselves to high standards that can be unachievable. We want to be sure we are not doing this to our spouse. Not only is it unfair to them, but to us as well!

It's Harder to Love Yourself Than to Accept Love From Others

Sometimes we rely too much on outside sources for our validation. In marriages and relationships this can easily happen. There is a term for this as well, called *codependency*.

Codependency is the mental, emotional, physical, and/or spiritual reliance on a partner, friend, or family member.

In relationships, codependency is often unhealthy and causes a loss of self, constant anxiety, and an almost obsessive dynamic between two people. Some questions to ask if you feel you or your partner may be codependent:

- *Do you constantly put your partner's needs above your own?*
- *Do you feel anxious if you cannot control a situation with your partner?*
- *Are you always struggling to find time for yourself?*
- *Have you stopped doing things you used to like?*
- *Do you need to constantly check in with your partner about things and feel unable to decide without them?*
- *Do you feel you've lost your sense of self?*
- *Do you feel a need to be liked by other people to feel good about yourself?*

If any of these are resonating with you, then you may be codependent. This is great to be aware of because you can work on ways to separate yourself from your partner. Again, this has no reflection on your feelings or love toward them. But this is a reason to work on your self love.

Codependency can lead to negative coping mechanisms, such as anxiety, depression, and substance abuse. Working on our self-love will not only improve our marriage, but it will improve our recognition of ourselves as a person.

Learning to Be Your Own Best Friend

Marriage is an incredible experience. It adds to our life, bringing us joy and love. Learning to love ourselves in the same way that we love our spouse teaches us a crucial life skill: how to be our own best friend! Life can be tough. No one will deny this! And, sometimes, there are things we deal with alone.

This could be for many reasons, but how do you react when situations like this arise? Are you kind to yourself? Do you treat yourself with the same compassion that you do with your spouse? These are important questions. Ultimately, this life is our journey. If we cannot play the role of our own best friend sometimes, then who will?

We now understand *why* it's important to love ourselves, but now how do we do it? We want to implement this as soon as possible. Recognizing how negative thought patterns within our minds and changing them will help us do the same outwardly. These next steps can be done all at the same time or can be used only when necessary! You will know what is best for yourself.

Quieting/Replacing Your Inner Voice

We all have an internal dialogue going on most of the time. We are always talking to ourselves whether we recognize it at the moment. *Is your inner voice a positive or negative one? Do you get down on yourself when you make a slight mistake? Do you always feel you are not good enough? How do you speak to yourself?*

This first step connects to the "Silver Rule" we discussed. The way we talk to ourselves is how we will talk to/view other people around us. But silencing that inner voice can be hard, and a negative inner voice can be automatic, like any other habit we have in our life.

We want to fight back against the voice and retrain our automatic thought process. Try this exercise:

If you normally think: *I can't believe I messed up. I'm so bad at everything.*
Try instead: *I messed up. But next time, I'll do better.*

OR

If you normally think: *I don't want to try that. I'll just fail, anyway.*
Try instead: *I'll give it a go. It will be an enjoyable experience!*

So much of how we view the world is perspective. If our inner dialogue is constantly negative and we talk down to ourselves, there's a good chance we will view the world the same way and eventually do so to our partners. Try some self-awareness for a while and stay conscious of those automatic thoughts. Be patient as you do, because any habit takes time to form and will take just as much time, if not more, to break.

Make Time for You

We have already covered this topic in-depth earlier in the chapter, but making time for yourself does not mean you always have to be working on yourself either. Give yourself a break! If you have a high-pressure job during the day, make sure you are allowing yourself the time to destress and relax in whatever way that looks like for you.

Everyone is different and will need more or less time to destress. You will know what is best. But once you do, honor that! Don't push yourself to the point of exhaustion because then you are setting yourself up for all kinds of other issues to creep in.

Set Healthy Boundaries

While we already discussed this in Chapter 3, boundaries are important for separating yourself from your partnership. Boundaries allow you to do things like work on your inner dialogue and spend time alone. Without them, you could easily find yourself in an unhealthy dynamic, such as a codependent relationship.

The boundaries we set in our lives are not just for others around us. This is important to note. Sometimes we cannot control how our spouse will react to something and we have to accept how they choose to, whether we like it. Here, we have to set a boundary for ourselves. A boundary is much like a choice. We are constantly making little decisions whether we are aware of it. And much of the world is our perception. So, what if we decide to work on that reaction? This could improve our self-awareness, confidence, and eventually the communication within our marriage.

Working on ourselves as an individual can feel like a tedious task. I know when I started doing this in my way; it was difficult for me to see how this could benefit the marriage. But then I found I stopped getting into minor arguments, deciding what was worth fighting over and what wasn't! I found other, positive things to focus my energy on, and I worked on getting back to the person I used to love and who my partner loves as well.

Again, this chapter is not about changing who you are deep down, but about getting back to that person! We can stray so far from ourselves in all aspects of our lives, but especially in a partnership with someone we love! It's admirable to love someone and care for them enough to put their needs before our own, but we do not want to forsake our sense of self entirely to do so.

Chapter Summary

- Making the relationship 50% better by working on yourself

- Self-love within a marriage is not selfish
- How to work on loving yourself

In the next chapter, you will learn how to move forward in your marriage with these communication skills.

6

MOVING FORWARD & MAINTAINING YOUR HEALTHY MARRIAGE

Armed with these tools and techniques, you are ready to move forward in your marriage. Understand that using these techniques will take time and can be done in steps. You may ask now how you can maintain the marriage? *Can this be done just by continuously using the principles?* The quick answer is yes. But we also want to keep our focus in the right place in the marriage. We want to keep that spark alive!

It feels like this is one of the most common questions surrounding couples. *How do we keep that spark going?* As we've seen in this book, maintaining a marriage is about so much more than just keeping a spark going. It's about communication, mutual understanding, and strengthening trust.

Hopefully, you feel armed with some tools to go forward and do just that. But, it's also good to think of how to keep that spark alive. *How do you and your partner do this?* Do you have a weekly date night? Or maybe there is even something the two of you do daily that brings you closer. Every couple is different and will have alternate ways to keep that spark alive in their marriage, but there is one thing they can all agree on.

Once the "honeymoon" stage is over, it's difficult to not long for it to come back. Throughout a marriage, life can get in the way and complicate things, making the marriage more of a business contract rather than a romantic one. This is a natural progression of the relationship, as your partner is someone you have gone through these life milestones with. You trust their judgments and ideas. But we can have both the romantic and business side of the relationship.

There are several tips to bring back that spark if you feel it has dissipated within your marriage.

1. Date Each Other

When you first meet someone, dating is an exciting aspect of the relationship. You can get ready, go out to dinner or a movie, and slowly get to know the person. Part of the excitement is the anticipation and waiting for the next time you see them. It's also nice just to spend time with someone you care about!

When couples have been married for a long time, they may cease dating each other altogether. Many couples think, *Well, we're married so why would we keep dating?* And while this makes sense, continuing to date can be a great way to share new experiences with your partner and show that you still care about them.

Remember that feeling of going to dinner for the first time with your partner? There were some endorphins and adrenaline involved. These are positive emotions, one that are healthy chemicals for romantic interest. Dating each other can help activate these in the brain again, and reactivate that spark.

2. Intimacy

Couples who are extremely busy with work or children may find that they have less time for intimacy. But intimacy is important for both physical and emotional connection. Try planning a special night for you and your partner to reconnect.

The need for intimacy is also something that will be different in every relationship, so this is somewhere where you can use the principles to communicate with your partner and ensure their needs and wants are being met.

3. Being Present

Sometimes our partners just want us to be there. Maybe there is something that your partner always asks for the two of you to do together, but you just won't do it. Or vice versa! Whatever it is, try engaging in that thing together.

Making the conscious choice to be present is a great way to show your partner you care. They will also notice, as we can feel when someone is truly listening to us vs. when they are just listening because they feel they have to.

4. Love as Action

Deciding to love our partner is harder than it seems. Love is a verb, and it means that we must consciously do it. Love is much like the relationship itself. It needs constant care, acknowledgment, and attention to work. This isn't something that just happens all by itself!

Keeping that spark alive is tough! But these tips will help you relight the flame. And you know your partner best. *What things do they like to do? What foods do they like? Is there a genre of movies they enjoy watching?* There are so many ways to recreate the honeymoon dynamic. Just keep the goal in mind! You want to strengthen the bond with your partner and decide that the marriage is worth putting in the hard work for.

We Get What We Allow

Something to note in all areas of our life is that we will always receive what we allow. If we allow things that make us unhappy to continue, then they will. If we allow miscommunication in our marriage, then there will be miscommunication. Seems simple, right? It's usually much more complex than this. But noting that we can make a change will get us where we need to ultimately be.

Certainly, you can pinpoint people in your life who behave in a certain way with you and differently with others. Why is this? For example, you have a friend who is never late to meet you for dinner or drinks, yet you always hear about how they are late to meet other people. Now the quick answer to this may be because they just like you better and care for you more than a friend! But the truth may be something else.

Think about this for a moment. Maybe they showed up late once a long time ago. And when they did, you told them you dislike that, and you would no longer see them if they showed up late again. By doing so, you showed them you will not tolerate or allow this behavior within your relationships.

This can be used in our marriage. While it does not need to be an ultimatum, often it just needs to be a conversation. Think about something your spouse does that drives you crazy. Maybe they are late all the time. Or, maybe they never change the bed sheets or Windex the bathroom mirror. Whatever it is, try using this technique with them. You could say: "I will no longer be Windexing the bathroom mirror unless you do it once a month." Their reaction will tell you a lot about their willingness to work on your marriage.

Just as important as tolerating certain behaviors from others, you need to have the same expectations for yourself. If you dislike when your partner is late, then you cannot be late. If you hate when they walk in the house with their shoes on, your shoes better be off at that front door!

Marriage is a two-way street! And we need to expect the same from ourselves. Also, if we are being lax on our actions, but expecting so much from others, we may subconsciously give leeway to those in our lives because we know we are not upholding those standards.

It's a tricky cycle, but we want to only tolerate what is healthy for us. From now on, deciding habitual patterns that will improve and not hinder the marriage is what will make all the difference.

How to Say Thank You

While we all learn to say thank you at a young age, this skill dissipates. We find less of a need to say thank you and it becomes automatic that we complete certain tasks and that our spouse completes others. Ask yourself at this moment, when was the last time you said thank you to your spouse? What did they do for you that made you say this? Do you think you could thank them for more things?

Even if it's something small, saying thank you can maintain the proper communication we put in place using the principles. It reiterates that we appreciate the effort our spouse is putting in for us and our relationship. It may feel weird to just begin saying "Thank you" often to your spouse, so here is an exercise to try!

Tell your partner you would like to write some things you are thankful that the other one does. You should both write a list and then share it with the other. This can illuminate, as there may be things you do you didn't know were important to your spouse! Getting all of this out on the table will only improve your communication and remind you and your partner how thankful you are to have one another.

Benefits of Saying Thank You

There are so many benefits of being appreciative toward our spouse. Showing anyone that we love and care for them will benefit the relationship. Just using these two words can increase your bond and bring you and your partner closer together. Let's look at some additional benefits:

1. A Shift in Perspective

We will be able to clearly see all that our partner does for us when we take note and thank them for it. They will do the same with us. Sometimes we don't always see what the other person does in the marriage and all it takes. Maybe you do all the housework, but they do the outdoor work (such as lawn care, gardening, etc.) Or, maybe you work a full-time job and your partner works part time.

An interesting exercise would be to switch for a couple of days, or even just a day. This way, you could see all that your spouse does and they could do the same for you. This would allow both of you a stronger appreciation of how you both work to make your partnership work together.

2. Better Communication

This entire book comprises effective ways to better communicate! This is yet another way to do so. Thanking our partner allows us to reflect on the meaning of our partner's efforts and therefore understand them better.

We also communicate that we recognize their efforts with just two small words. *Isn't it amazing what just two words can say?* I think this is a testament to spoken language and communication overall.

3. Healthier Pattern Formation

We have talked about breaking down old habits and working to form new ones. Saying thank you is a great habit to get into. Before you know it, it will become an automatic way to show appreciation to your spouse. It will even be an easy habit to start. It is only two words! And your partner may pick up on this and start doing the same thing.

4. Open the Door for Healing

If we have been repressing and lacking in communicating with our spouse, saying thank you can open the door to healing and larger conversation. As I have stated, many marriages repress things for an alarming amount of time. This means that communication is lacking by default and there is no space for healing.

How can we possibly know what is bothering our partner if they have let it simmer for so long? Conversely, how can we expect our partners to be open to fixing something if they know nothing is wrong? While "Thank you" is only two small words, the implication and deeper meaning is enough to start a productive dialogue between you and your spouse.

These are just a few benefits of showing how much our spouse means to us. But, the biggest benefit is that "Thank You" slowly turns into "I love you." Another thing that happens in a marriage after some time is "I love you's" to get reserved for certain occasions. Maybe they are uttered briefly when they are running out of the house for work in the morning or before major life events. This is not enough! Maybe this doesn't apply to your marriage, and that's okay! But if it does, implementing phrases like "I love you" will make you appreciate your spouse in alternative ways and will help you back to other phrases such as "I love you" more naturally.

Maintaining Without Arguing

Many couples argue. It's just a common phrase you hear around couples whenever they disagree. But there is a big difference between arguing and working out a core conflict. And, you are now ready to move forward in your marriage! You want to use healthier ways to solve issues. All couples will have problems, whether they are married. What you want to do is ensure that you are moving forward in a direction that benefits both you and your partner.

Life's a rollercoaster! There will be difficulties. There will be times when you feel very connected with your partner and other times when you feel like the spark might be gone for good. But it's so important to maintain your relationship without arguing because arguing will get you nowhere. Here are some fast reasons to never argue with your spouse:

- It's not productive
- You don't want to say something you regret
- It could escalate to something more
- You and your spouse will not hear one another

There is a big difference between arguing and discussing. Arguing includes yelling your side at your spouse while they yell their side of you. This is just a waste of time. The principles will help you have discussions about sensitive subjects and things that may bother both of you, and resolve them healthily.

Chapter Summary

- Tips to move forward
- We get what we allow
- How to say thank you and correlated benefits
- Maintaining without arguing

CONCLUSION

Hopefully, you feel armed with some tools and techniques that you can use in your marriage. No marriage is perfect. I know I have said this throughout this book, but it is good to remind yourself of this. We don't want to think that we are the only ones going through this struggle because all married couples struggle. It's just part of life! But the beautiful part of marriage is that you get to have someone along with you on that life journey.

Communication is crucial for all human interactions. When we have been with someone for so long, we take this for granted. It can be assumed that they know what we are thinking and feeling at all times, but no one, not even our spouse, is a mind reader. There are many forms of communication that we discussed, such as verbal, nonverbal, emotional, and touch. You will know which one is the most important in your marriage.

Remember to not get sucked into the myths of marriage. We went over several myths that are so common you may have already believed them! This lack of communication within your marriage can have devastating effects, and hopefully, you've found the principles in this book helped you remove the guesswork and instead use direct communication.

The core conflicts you and your partner face are the same that other couples face. While they take different shapes and forms, at the root is the same issue! Once we can see these issues, you can stop adding conflict to conflict by avoiding and arguing with your partner.

You can use the STRENGTHEN 10-Principle Guide at any point. You can bring it with you in the car, your purse, backpack, dresser drawer. You never know when you'll need it! The principles are extremely useful because you can use them one at a time or all at once. Knowing yourself is crucial for these principles because only you and your partner can decide which ones will benefit you the most. Keep in mind that time is precious! You and your partner chose each other for a reason and your time is more valuable than anything.

Healthy boundaries within yourself and your marriage can be just the thing to fix those core conflicts. You learn what you will tolerate within your relationship and what you want. Remember this if nothing else: Your marriage is the Other thing to yourself. And you may set boundaries when you feel yourself being compromised.

You cannot save the marriage by yourself, but you can work on yourself to make the marriage 50% better. Each partner has to do their point to make the marriage stronger. A self-love is never a selfish act in a partnership. We want to be the best version of ourselves that we can be for our partners!

There are simple things we can start doing right now to make the relationship better. Even adding two words to our rhetoric: "Thank you." This is such a simple phrase that shows our partner we acknowledge what they are doing and care enough to show appreciation for it. So much of marriage is appreciation! Our partners should know that we see them, and we see what they do every day to make our partnership work. Also, we want them to see the same for us.

We want to maintain this marriage with productive discussions that uplift and improve our marriage, not hinder it. The real-life examples in this book show you are not alone, and the marriage statistics also helped show you what most people find important in their marriage.

While every marriage is different, it's clear that these core issues are found in most partnerships. But, we can solve them! You have taken this step and by doing so have already improved your situation. You are ready to use these tools in your situation now, strengthen your trust, and improve the communication within your marriage day by day.

ACKNOWLEDGMENTS

Dear Reader,
Thank you for reading my book.
I hope you enjoyed the journey together and found this book helpful.
If so, please leave a review. Your feedback is essential for me to improve, and it will help other people know how this book can help them as well.

Thank you
Caroline Sowle

Made in the USA
Coppell, TX
11 February 2022